The Medico-Legal Development of Neurological Death in the UK

Kartina A. Choong

The Medico-Legal Development of Neurological Death in the UK

Springer

Kartina A. Choong
School of Justice
University of Central Lancashire
Preston, UK

ISBN 978-981-19-6762-7 ISBN 978-981-19-6763-4 (eBook)
https://doi.org/10.1007/978-981-19-6763-4

This Springer imprint is published by the registered company Springer Nature Singapore Pte Ltd.
The registered company address is: 152 Beach Road, #21-01/04 Gateway East, Singapore 189721, Singapore

This book is dedicated to my mother and the memory of my father

Preface

Diagnosis of death using neurological criteria (DNC) is a construct which has been part of the medico-legal discourse for around half a century. This book examines its historical evolution in the UK from medical and legal perspectives.

Chapter 1 traces the origin of the concept to the wider use of mechanical ventilation in modern intensive care units in Europe and the USA, and explores the manner in which its development was connected to the field of organ transplantation. Chapter 2 discusses the extent to which events in Europe and the USA influenced the uptake of DNC in the UK. It investigates the factors behind its emergence and discusses the various changes that took place in the last few decades that culminated in the current definition and criteria for determining brain-based death. Also highlighted are the continuities and discontinuities in practice and the impact they have on the issue of withdrawal of mechanical ventilation in ICUs and on the field of organ transplantation. In Chap. 3, the law's response to the introduction and development of DNC in clinical practice will be analysed. It will demonstrate how the legitimacy of the definition and criteria used by the medical profession was forged in the courtroom rather than Parliamentary chambers. It explores why case law was introduced in court and assesses whether organ donation was a consideration in the deliberations. It will be highlighted that courts have given short shrift to requests made in recent cases to consider a broader range of methods to determine death. The chapter concludes by drawing attention to the trends and tendencies that have emerged over time. Chapter 4 begins by taking a close look at the issues sidelined by the courts, namely that the definition and criteria espoused by the medical profession in the UK are dissimilar to those used in other jurisdictions that also adopt DNC and that faith communities have a different understanding of death. This chapter illustrates the inherent limitations of the courtroom as the forum for forging the legitimacy of DNC. It puts forward the argument that the democratic process should instead be engaged, by reviewing the comparative advantage of Parliamentary law-making. Chapter 5 looks back at DNC's medico-legal journey to date, before looking ahead to the future.

Preston, UK Kartina A. Choong

The original version of the book was revised: Corrections have been updated in all the chapter XML. The correction to the book is available at https://doi.org/10.1007/978-981-19-6763-4_6

Acknowledgements

My first expression of gratitude goes to the late Sahin Aksoy for triggering my interest in the topic. Since then, my thinking on DNC has also benefitted from discussions with Mahmood Chandia, Mohamed Rady, Michael Salter and the attendees of several Medical Law and Bioethics conferences. For responding to my queries and sending over helpful materials, I thank Peter Elsner, Roslyn Jones, Akiko Kogawara and Vincent Maher. I would also like to thank Louise Smith from UCLan Library and Customer Services for helping me locate a number of important resources and the Law School for funding my research at the Wellcome Library in London.

This book was completed during the COVID-19 pandemic. For the different ways in which they have helped make this challenging time more manageable, I am very grateful to Henrik Andersen, Ali Ashtiani, Ava Ashtiani, Shareen Edwards, Steve Edwards, Julie Farrer, Mark Gaskell, Susan Hancock, Gill Hoyle, Shalini Kanagasingam, Richard Law, Tina McKee, Munira Patel, Richard Saffrey-Mayger, Evelyn Salaverria, Mohamed Salem Abou El Farag, Abhay Vaidya, Hugh Williams and Yinan Yin.

To my family, thank you for your patience and understanding, particularly when the international travel restrictions were in place.

Contents

About the Author

Dr. Kartina A. Choong is a Reader in Medical Law and Ethics at the University of Central Lancashire (UCLan), having previously held academic appointments at the universities of Durham, Reading and Leeds Metropolitan. She has served as Subject Specialist for Medical Ethics and Religion for INTUTE: Arts and Humanities (formerly the HUMBUL Humanities Hub based at the University of Oxford) (2002–2010) and sat on the *British Medical Journal* (BMJ)'s Ethics Committee (2018–2021).

She obtained her Law degree from the University of Cardiff before qualifying as a Barrister (Honourable Society of Lincoln's Inn, London). She holds master's degrees in Healthcare Ethics and Applied Social Research from the University of Manchester and in Islamic Studies from the University of Leeds. Her Ph.D. in Medical Law was awarded by the University of Manchester. Her main areas of research interests, on which she has published widely, include neurological death, medical futility, religiously and culturally sensitive end-of-life care, palliative care, medical mediation, professional liability, access to health records, consent and confidentiality.

Abbreviations

BBC	British Broadcasting Corporation
BPA	British Paediatric Association
DDR	Dead Donor Rule
DNC	Death by Neurological Criteria
EEG	Electroencephalogram
HTA	Human Tissue Authority
ICU	Intensive Care Unit
LST	Life-sustaining Treatment
NHS	National Health Service
RCP	Royal College of Physicians
RCPCH	Royal College of Paediatrics and Child Health
UDDA	Uniform Determination of Death Act
UK	United Kingdom of Great Britain and Northern Ireland
USA	United States of America
WMA	World Medical Association

List of Cases

Aintree University Hospitals NHS Foundation Trust v. James [2013] UKSC 67
Airedale NHS Trust v. Bland [1993] AC 789
Alder Hey Children's NHS Foundation Trust v. Evans, James and Evans [2018] EWHC 953 (Fam)
An NHS Trust and Others v. Y and Another [2018] UKSC 46
Barts Health NHS Trust v. Dance, Battersbee and Battersbee [2022] EWCA Civ 935
Barts Health NHS Trust v. Dance, Battersbee and Battersbee [2022] EWFC 80
Barts Health NHS Trust v. Dance, Battersbee and Battersbee [2022] EWHC 1435 (Fam)
C (By His Father and Litigation Friend 'F') v. North Cumbria University Hospitals NHS Trust [2014] EWHC 61 (QB)
Cleveland County Council v. F and Others [1995] 1 WLR 785
Dance and Battersbee v. Barts Health NHS Trust and Battersbee [2022] EWCA Civ 1055
Fonseca v. Kaiser Permanent Medical Center Roseville and Others, Case No. 2:16-CV-60889-KJM-EFB (2016)
Great Ormond Street Hospital v. Yates, Gard and Gard [2017] EWHC 1909 (Fam)
Manchester University NHS Foundation Trust v. Namiq, Ali and Namiq [2020] EWHC 5 (Fam)
McKitty v. Hayani, 2019 ONCA 805
Nakar v. New York Presbyterian Hospital, Columbia University Irving Medical Center and Milstein Pavilion Medical Intensive Care Unit, No. 1780/2017 (Kings County Supreme Court, NY, 2019)
Ouanounou v. Humber River Hospital et al. 2017 ONSC 651
Oxford University NHS Trust v. AB (A Minor), CD and EF [2019] EWHC 3516 (Fam)
P.P. v. Health Service Executive [2014] IEHC 622
R v. Her Majesty's Coroner for Coventry 2000 WL 989473
R v. Malcherek; R v. Steel (1981) 73 Cr. App. R. 173
R v. Morrison (Ian Stuart) [2003] EWCA Crim 1953

R (John Smeaton on Behalf of Society for the Protection of Unborn Children) v. The Secretary of State for Health v. Schering Health Care Ltd, Family Planning Association [2002] EWHC 610 (Admin)
R (On the Application of Nicklinson and Another) v. Ministry of Justice [2014] UKSC 38
Re A (A Child) [2015] EWHC 443
Re A (A Minor) [1992] 3 Med L.R. 303
Re M (Declaration of Death of Child) [2020] EWCA Civ 164
Winkfield v. Children's Hospital and Research Center at Oakland, California Northern District Court Oakland Division, Case No. C 13-05993 (2013)

Chapter 1
Death Revisited

Abstract Death has traditionally been determined on the basis of the cessation of heartbeat and breathing. The last few decades witnessed the emergence of the neurological determination of death. This chapter traces its origin to the wider use of mechanical ventilation in modern intensive care units, and explores the manner in which its development was connected to the field of organ transplantation. The chapter ends by highlighting the public unease which can be discerned from the legal developments in some jurisdictions.

Keywords Mechanical ventilation · Coma *dépassé* · Harvard criteria · Intensive care units · Organ transplantation · Diagnosis of death using neurological criteria

1.1 Introduction

Death is a concept that has no universal definition and it has been described in a myriad of ways. A person who is dead is often thought of as having, among others, "left this world", "passed away", "departed", "passed on" or "expired".[1] For decades or even centuries heretofore, death seemed to have been diagnosed using solely cardio-respiratory criteria.[2] When this had been the case, determining whether breathing and heartbeat have ceased did not appear to have been a complex nor a contentious matter. Just as no sophisticated equipment had been necessary to help one to reach this conclusion, neither was there any need for specialist medical training to make that diagnosis.[3] Death was concluded upon simple physical observations. These range from something as rudimentary as the failure to get up after being called three times, to the more conventional ones like the absence of fog on a mirror placed under nostrils, the absence of movement when a feather or a piece of straw was placed in front of the mouth or nose, the absence of a pulse, and the lack of spontaneous movements and unresponsiveness to stimuli.[4] Similarly if the diagnosis had been

[1] Devettere (2010), p. 134; Hutchison (2008), p. 438.

[2] Laureys and Fins (2008) at e14.

[3] Ackerknecht (1968) at 19.

[4] Sarbey (2016) at 743–744; Machado (2007), p. 1; Prioreschi (1996), p. 29; Daniel (1997), p. 41.

K. A. Choong, *The Medico-Legal Development of Neurological Death in the UK*,
https://doi.org/10.1007/978-981-19-6763-4_1

made by physicians, these had needed only clinical observations[5] which were often conducted without any standard criteria.[6] The initial diagnosis, if correct, was soon accompanied by other indicators like a drop in body temperature, stiffness, paleness and subsequently by putrefaction and emission of an unpleasant odour.[7]

This traditional conception, the idea that death is associated with the cessation of breathing and heartbeat, nevertheless came under critical scrutiny in the early years after the Second World War. This was prompted by the rising use of mechanical ventilation within modern intensive care units (ICUs). Although the impetus for this has often been attributed to the 1952 Copenhagen poliomyelitis epidemic, mechanical ventilation—the device which aims to substitute physiological respiratory function—has already been in use particularly in the latter half of the nineteenth century and the first half of the twentieth century.[8] These were predominantly negative pressure ventilators, which operate by reducing the ambient pressure around the thorax.[9]

By contrast, the Copenhagen poliomyelitis epidemic used positive pressure ventilation. This form of ventilation operates by increasing the pressure within the airways.[10] It had hitherto been confined to the operating room.[11] However, this changed when the Blegdam Hospital (*Blegdamshospitalet*) had to admit around 3000 patients diagnosed with poliomyelitis in the last 5 months of 1952, several hundred of whom with respiratory insufficiency and bulbar palsy.[12] When the hospital's limited supply of negative pressure ventilators proved inadequate in assisting all the patients who needed respiratory support, many of them died including child patients. The hospital's anaesthetist, Dr. Bjørn Ibsen, was consulted. Upon his suggestion, manual intermittent positive pressure ventilation, a common anaesthetic technique used in the operating theatre at the time, was implemented.[13] Tracheotomies were performed

---

[5] The last few centuries have seen the use of mechanisms like the Magnus test (where a string was tied firmly around a supposed corpse's finger to see if circulation was still maintained in which case the whole finger would swell); the Diaphanous test (where the hand of a supposedly dead person was placed before a strong artificial light and the person was pronounced dead in the absence of a scarlet line of light in the narrow spaces between the fingers as that was believed to signify circulation); and the stethoscope to detect the absence of heartbeat—see Stone (1872), p. 111; Lawrence (1893), p. 1250; and Gardiner et al. (2012).

[6] Greer (2020) at 1079.

[7] Hayman and Oxenham (2016), pp. 1–4; Mant (1987), p. 66; American Academy of Orthopaedic Surgeons (2005), p. 83.

[8] Romero-Ávila et al. (2020) at 822.

[9] Young and Sykes (1990) at 753. The subatmospheric (or negative) pressure leads to thoracic expansion and a corresponding decrease in pleural and alveolar pressures. These create a pressure gradient for air to move from the airway opening into the alveoli. Expiration then takes place when the pressure surrounding the thorax increases and becomes atmospheric—Corrado and Gorini (2002) at pp. 187–188.

[10] Expiration of air takes place passively secondary to the build up of pressure in the alveoli which escapes into the less pressurised conductive airways—Brown and Roberts (2019) at 72.

[11] Where it was used during general anaesthesia to simulate the normal human respiratory pattern and restore near normal gas exchange—see MacIntyre et al. (2021) at 559.

[12] Lassen (1954) at 67.

[13] Pincock (2007) at 1538; Trubuhovich (2003) at 227.

below the larynx of such patients and rubber cuff tubes were inserted into their tracheas, with positive pressure ventilation from rubber bags (bag ventilation). This was used on a massive scale requiring over 1000 volunteer medical, dental and nursing students, as well as semi-retired nurses, to work in shifts to provide manual respiration round the clock.[14] As a result, there was a dramatic reduction in the mortality rate from 80 to 23%.[15]

Further, when those patients were placed in a dedicated department where every patient could have their own nurse, this also heralded the beginning of ICUs as they are known today.[16] Although the idea of concentrating the most seriously ill or injured patients proximal to the nursing station so that they can be observed more closely is often traced further back to Florence Nightingale during the Crimean War of the 1850s, this initiative and other ICUs in the next 100 years were generally physical sites which accommodated primarily postoperative patients for special and personalised care.[17] The intensive care provided was essentially intensive nursing care.[18] By contrast, contemporary ICUs are technology-dependent. In addition to mechanical ventilators, they also house a range of other equipment including monitoring systems, ultrasound machines, dialysis machines, intravenous lines and pumps, breathing tubes, feeding tubes, drains and catheters.[19] Together, the devices and techniques help monitor patients' health and support their bodily functions. These specialist wards are now staffed by highly trained specialised staff who deliver intensive levels of care and treatment. These include Consultants in Intensive Care Medicine, medical doctors, nurses, and allied health professionals like physiotherapists, occupational therapists, clinical pharmacists, dieticians, speech and language therapists, respiratory therapists, and clinical psychologists.[20]

Meanwhile, the success of the ventilatory technique used at Blegdam Hospital also prompted a changeover from manual to mechanical, longer term intermittent positive pressure ventilation throughout the Scandinavia and other parts of the world.[21] Temporary breathing tubes placed through the mouth (intubation) supplanted surgical tracheotomy.[22] Housed in modern ICUs, mechanical ventilators soon assumed a prominent role in the management of patients with severe respiratory failure owing to a range of conditions.

Mechanical ventilation, when combined with the life-sustaining possibilities offered by the modern ICU, suggest that while the cessation of breathing and heartbeat

---

[14] West (2005) at 425–426.

[15] J. D. Young and M. K. Sykes, op. cit., p. 753.

[16] Kelly et al. (2014) at 376–377; Ibsen (1954) at 73. For a discussion of the development of ICUs elsewhere in Europe and the USA, see Wijdicks et al. (2011).

[17] Vincent (2013); Weil and Tang (2011) at 1451.

[18] Marshall et al. (2017) at 270.

[19] NHS, 'Intensive Care', available at https://www.nhs.uk/conditions/intensive-care/; Lichtenstein (2014).

[20] Anandaciva (2020); Ervin et al. (2018).

[21] R. V. Trubuhovich, op. cit., p. 228.

[22] Wertheim (2020).

would previously be indicative of the end of human life, these can now be reversed and regulated mechanically. This capability soon raised an intractable dilemma. If the human respiratory system and cardiac functions can be sustained mechanically, how long should ventilation be maintained? In some cases, it was clear that this can be ended when the patient regained consciousness. However, in situations where doctors realised that the patient's condition was hopeless but life support perpetuated bodily functions, does the then prevailing assumption that life support must be provided until someone was dead, still apply?[23] This question eventually led to the quest for diagnostic criteria, which when satisfied, would enable the switching off of the mechanical ventilator and the withdrawal of life-sustaining treatment (LST). This, in time, gave rise to a new definition of death.

1.2 The Birth of Neurological Death

1.2.1 Coma Dépassé

In 1959, two French neurophysiologists, Pierre Mollaret (1898–1987) and Maurice Goulon (1919–2008), published an article describing the condition of 23 patients whom they were treating at the Claude Bernard Hospital in Paris.[24] Those patients, having suffered massive brain injuries and maintained on ventilators, were unresponsive to external stimuli and were incontinent; and had lost the ability to swallow and control their body temperature and blood pressure. Further, they had lost their tendon reflexes as well as their ocular responses to light and touch, and were recognised as having no discernible electrical activity in the brains.[25] These patients were found to be in an irreversible state of coma and apnoea.

At the time, there had seemed to be three degrees of coma that were recognised by the scientific community. These were the classical coma (characterised by the loss of relational life functions like consciousness, mobility, sensibility and reflexes); an alert coma (where the loss of relational functions was not complete); and a *carus* coma (where the preservation of vegetative life was seriously threatened).[26] To these 3 known phenomenology of the coma, Mollaret and Goulon proposed to add the condition afflicting the 23 patients as another category of coma (i.e. a coma in which the total abolition of relational life functions corresponds to an equally total abolition of vegetative life functions) to distinguish it from other types of comatose states.[27] Those patients were described as being in a *coma dépassé*, which has been translated

[23] Veatch (2018) at S6.

[24] Mollaret and Goulon (1959).

[25] Evans (2000) at 144.

[26] Agamben (2017), p. 132.

[27] Wijdicks (2017), p. 5.

as "ultra-coma", "death of the brain",[28] '"fourth degree coma",[29] "a state beyond coma",[30] "irreversible coma",[31] "excessive coma",[32] "overcoma"[33] or "beyond the deepest coma so far described."[34]

According to them, this condition was characterised by "immobility of the eyeballs in a neutral position, mydriasis, absent light reflex, absent blinking with stimuli, absence of swallowing reflexes, drooping of the jaw, absence of motor responses to any stimuli, muscle hypotonia, tendon are flexia, equivocal plantar reflexes, absence of spontaneous respiration after discontinuation of ventilation, immediate cardiovascular collapse as soon as vasopressors are stopped, and a disturbance of thermoregulation with core temperature, depending on the environmental temperature."[35] Mollaret and Goulon raised the question of whether it is appropriate to withdraw ventilation and LST from such patients as the prognosis had seemed extremely poor. It was believed that *coma dépassé* was incompatible with neurologic recovery.[36] As those patients were deemed as still being alive rather than dead, their concern had seemed centred around not wanting to prolong the dying process, for what was considered futile intervention.[37]

While the issue was of immense interest to those managing the new and emerging ICUs, *coma dépassé* was also of enormous interest to those involved in organ transplantation.[38] Although transplant medicine has made great strides since the early 1900s,[39] it was not until the 1960s that vital organs like heart, lungs, liver and pancreas began to be successfully transplanted.[40] This development prompted the conception of the dead donor rule (DDR).[41] This is the formalisation of the commonly held belief that it is wrong to kill one person to save another person's life.[42] The donors of vital organs should therefore first be declared dead before those organs are procured, since their removal from living persons will certainly bring about their demise.[43] For that reason, those organs were procured from patients who had died of cardiac death,

---

28 Jonsen (1998), p. 237.

29 D.W. Evans, op. cit., p. 144.

30 Pearson (1995) at 11.

31 Pontificia Academia Pro Vita Assembly, 'The Dignity of the Dying', p. 427.

32 Zhu and Han (2021) p. 2.

33 G. Agamben, op. cit., p. 132.

34 Wijdicks (2013a) at 191.

35 Wijdicks (2013b) p. 100.

36 Munoz and Fox (2013) at 22.

37 Kalitzkus (2004) at 146; Gross et al. (2019) at 190.

38 A.R. Jonsen, op. cit., p. 237.

39 Schlich (2011) at 1373. For discussion of earlier interest and initiatives in tissue and organ transplantation, see e.g. Hamilton (2012), Chapters 1 and 2; Crawford et al. (2013); Sturgis (1942).

40 Watson and Dark (2012) at i30.

41 Robertson (1999).

42 Sade (2011) at 146–147.

43 Kerridge et al. (2002) at 90.

the only recognised type of death then.[44] However, since organs retrieved from such patients would be deprived of blood and oxygen for a duration of time, they would not necessarily be in optimal condition for transplantation. This prompted doctors to discern the precise moment when prospective donors had died in order to remove organs in the best possible condition so as to increase the chances of a successful transplant.[45]

In 1966, at an international and interdisciplinary symposium organised by the Ciba Foundation to review transplantation ethics, it was proclaimed that shortage of organs was seriously impeding the life-saving and life-enhancing potential of transplantation. To expand the possible sources of homotransplants, one area that was looked at was the removal of tissues and organs from cadavers.[46] This prompted intense discussions as to whether *coma dépassé* could be equated with death for the purpose of organ procurement. As conflicting viewpoints were expressed, the symposium which was attended by most of the leading transplanters and researchers of the time,[47] concluded without reaching a consensus as to whether death should be redefined. The event nevertheless demonstrated that the interests of organ transplantation played an instrumental role in the subsequent reclassification of irreversible coma as death.[48]

1.2.2 The Harvard Criteria for Brain Death

A watershed moment took place in 1968 with the setting up of the *Ad Hoc* Committee of the Harvard Medical School to Examine the Definition of Brain Death. Chaired by Professor Henry Beecher (1904–1976), an American anaesthesiologist, the committee's primary purpose was to "define irreversible coma as a new criterion for death".[49] They explained that there are two reasons as to why a definition was needed: "(1) improvements in resuscitative and supportive measures have led to increased efforts to save those who are desperately injured. Sometimes these efforts have only partial success so that the result is an individual whose heart continues to beat but whose brain is irreversibly damaged. The burden is great on patients who suffer permanent loss of intellect, on their families, on the hospitals, and on those in need of hospital beds already occupied by these comatose patients. (2) Obsolete criteria for the definition of death can lead to controversy in obtaining organs for transplantation."[50]

---

[44] Nordham and Ninokawa (2022) at 126.

[45] Nipper (2017) at 433.

[46] Woodruff (1966) at 10.

[47] Jonsen (2012) at 264.

[48] Nguyen (2019a) at 44–46.

[49] *Ad Hoc* Committee of the Harvard Medical School to Examine the Definition of Brain Death (1968) at 85.

[50] Ibid.

The committee took the view that a brain that no longer functioned, and has no possibility of functioning again, was for all practical purposes dead. Limiting the remit of their task to "comatose individuals who have no discernible central nervous system activity",[51] patients in this state were described as having a "permanently nonfunctioning brain".[52] This could be diagnosed by satisfying the following 3 conditions[53]: unreceptivity and unresponsivity[54]; no movements or breathing[55]; and absence of elicitable reflexes.[56] In addition to the 3 conditions, it was highlighted that the electroencephalogram (EEG) should be used when available. A flat or isoelectric EEG is said to hold strong confirmatory value. Where electroencephalographic monitoring was not available, the absence of cerebral function was to be ascertained by purely clinical signals, to be described, or through the lack of circulation as ascertained by standstill of blood in the retinal vessels, or by absence of cardiac activity.[57]

All of the tests above are to be repeated at least 24 h later, with no change. That the data are valid indications of irreversible cerebral damage depends on the exclusion of hypothermia or central nervous system depressants. According to the committee, only a physician can determine the patient's condition.[58] Once death is declared, the ventilator is to be turned off. The decision to do this and the responsibility for doing so are to be shouldered by the physician-in-charge, in consultation with one or more physicians who have been directly involved in the patient's care.[59]

The *Ad Hoc* Committee published their report on 5th of August 1968 and those conditions for determining brain death were subsequently known as "the Harvard criteria".[60] Importantly, by giving irreversible coma a new name, and by defining it as a new criterion for death, the report catapulted brain death into clinical medicine.[61] It is nevertheless necessary to highlight that this new method of determining death was

---

51 Ibid.

52 Ibid.

53 Ibid., pp. 85–86.

54 I.e. complete unawareness to externally applied stimuli and inner need and complete unresponsiveness, so much so that even the most intensely painful stimuli evoke no response at all.

55 I.e. an absence of any spontaneous muscular movements or respiration or response to stimuli after being observed for at least an hour by physicians. After the patient was on artificial ventilator, the complete absence of spontaneous breathing may be ascertained by switching off the machine for 3 min and observe whether the patient made any effort to breathe spontaneously.

56 I.e. the pupil would be fixed, dilated and not responsive to a direct source of bright lights. Also absent are ocular movement to head turning and irrigation of the ears with ice water; blinking; postural activity; and corneal and pharyngeal reflexes. Swallowing, yawning and vocalisation are in abeyance; the stretch of tendon reflexes cannot be elicited; and plantar or noxious stimulation draws no response.

57 *Ad Hoc* Committee of the Harvard Medical School to Examine the Definition of Brain Death, op. cit., p. 86.

58 Ibid.

59 Ibid.

60 S. Laureys and J.J. Fins, op. cit., p. e14.

61 Nguyen (2019b) at 297–298.

not intended to replace the traditional cardio-respiratory method. Instead, what was negotiated and offered was a second pathway in which a specific subset of comatose patients—who were not dead under the traditional standard in that their hearts were still beating—could be declared dead under the new method, while remaining on artificial ventilation.[62] Crucially, the initiative enabled not only for ventilation to be removed from those "hopelessly damaged"[63] patients. It also cleared the way for the procurement of organs from patients with cardiac functions who have been pronounced brain dead but continue to receive artificial ventilation.[64]

Despite the monumental effect of its decision, the *Ad Hoc* Committee did not provide an explanation as to why brain death constituted death. This was offered, around a decade later, by the President's Commission for the Study of Ethical Problems in Medicine and Biomedical and Behavioral Research. According to the Commission, "death is that moment at which the body's physiological system ceases to constitute an integrated whole. Even if life continues in individual cells or organs, life of the organism as a whole requires complex integration, and without the latter, a person cannot properly be regarded as alive".[65] It took the view that the brain is the regulator or integrator of bodily functions—thus when the entire brain is dead, the organism no longer functions as an integrated whole, hence dead.[66] The Commission also investigated whether the law ought to recognise this new way of establishing that human death has occurred.[67] This was driven in part by concerns raised by doctors over the legal status of brain dead patients: are those patients legally dead before ventilators are switched off, and are prospective donors legally dead when vital organs are removed from their heart-beating ventilated bodies?[68] The Commission reported that death is a unitary phenomenon which can be accurately demonstrated on either one of two standards: the traditional grounds of irreversible cessation of heart and lung functions, or on the basis of irreversible loss of all functions of the entire brain.[69] Following its conclusion that the necessary changes in the law was best achieved through statute, the Harvard criteria were instantiated into law in the United States of America (USA) in 1981 with the adoption of the Uniform Determination of Death Act (UDDA).[70] This, which became a model for their 50 states to draft legislation defining brain death, stated that: "An individual who has sustained either (1) irreversible cessation of circulatory and respiratory functions, or (2) irreversible

[62] Nair-Collins (2022) at 43.

[63] *Ad Hoc* Committee of the Harvard Medical School to Examine the Definition of Brain Death, op. cit., p. 86.

[64] Sole et al. (2021), p. 36; Johnson (2016) at 107.

[65] President's Commission for the Study of Ethical Problems in Medicine and Biomedical and Behavioral Research, (1981), p. 33.

[66] Ibid., p. 35.

[67] President's Commission for the Study of Ethical Problems in Medicine and Biomedical and Behavioral Research (1983), p. 13.

[68] Capron (2018) at S14–S15; Miller and Truog (2012); Converse (1975) at 434–435.

[69] President's Commission for the Study of Ethical Problems in Medicine and Biomedical and Behavioral Research (1983), op. cit., p. 15 (emphasis added).

[70] Truog (2020) at S76.

cessation of all functions of the entire brain, including the brain stem, is dead. A determination of death must be made in accordance with accepted medical standard." The UDDA thus rendered brain death equivalent to traditional cardio-respiratory death.[71] Following this model, death can be determined upon the satisfaction of either standard. Thus if the irreversible cessation of all brain functions is confirmed, a patient may be declared dead despite ongoing cardiopulmonary functions maintained by mechanical ventilation or pharmacological support.[72]

1.3 Growth and Development

On the very same day that the Harvard *Ad Hoc* Committee published their report, the World Medical Association (WMA)'s World Medical Assembly met in Sydney, Australia[73] and issued the Declaration of Sydney on the Determination of Death and the Recovery of Organs.[74] The WMA is an international organisation which was founded soon after the Second World War, on 17 September 1947. It aims to promote the highest possible standard of medical ethics amongst physicians and provide ethical guidance through Declarations, Resolutions and Statements.[75] According to the Declaration of Sydney,[76] death can be determined on the basis of "the irreversible cessation of all functions of the entire brain, including the brain stem, or the irreversible cessation of circulatory and respiratory functions." This determination will be "based on clinical judgment according to accepted criteria, supplemented, if necessary, by standard diagnostic procedures, and it will be made by a physician". It highlighted that cell, organ and tissue activity may subsist after a determination of death. Hence cessation of all life at the cellular level is not a precondition of death. It added that for patients who are mechanically supported, such support may be maintained after death has been pronounced, in order to preserve organs and tissues for purposes of transplantation. The diagnosis and declaration of death shall be made by a physician who is not immediately involved in the transplantation procedure. Once death is confirmed, all treatment and resuscitation attempts may be halted, and organ retrieval may be commenced.

Diagnosis of death using neurological criteria (DNC) has since gained wider international recognition and acceptance. The United Kingdom (UK) was one of

---

71 Johnson (2017) at 267.

72 Pope (2015), p. 3.

73 Machado et al. (2007) at 699.

74 This Declaration has since been amended by the 35th World Medical Assembly in 1983; the 57th WMA General Assembly in 2006; and the 67th WMA General Assembly in 2016.

75 World Medical Association, 'About Us', available at https://www.wma.net/who-we-are/about-us/.

76 According to Machado et al., the Sydney and Harvard committees had actually worked in parallel "without either being aware of the other's work"—see Machado et. al., op. cit., p. 701. The WMA's study was prompted by similar concerns over (1) medicine's ability to maintain circulation by artificial means; and (2) the use of cadaver organs for transplantation—see Gilder (1968) at 493.

its earliest proponents. There are nevertheless inconsistencies among the countries which have embraced DNC on how death is defined. Some have made reference to whole-brain death.[77] Others, like the UK, refer to brain stem death.[78] Further, even among those that adopt the same definition, there are wide variations in the criteria, protocols and procedures used when determining death.[79] Notwithstanding these differences, the addition of neurological criteria of death to cardiorespiratory criteria of death was a paradigm shift which generated a hitherto inconceivable phenomenon.[80] For the first time in history, patients meeting the diagnostic criteria for death can still appear life-like in the most intuitive sense.[81] Notwithstanding the fact that they are immobile and no longer respond to their environment, they are still breathing and have a beating heart; their skin is warm to the touch; their wounds still heal; their hair still grow; they can menstruate; they can digest food, urinate and defecate; they can demonstrate quite complex spinal reflexes; and they can even gestate a foetus to term.[82]

So unique are these "living cadavers"[83] or "ventilated corpses"[84] that the hybridity created an inevitable chasm between the medical and the public understandings of death.[85] Although DNC gained acceptance over time, signs of public unease can be discerned from the legal developments in some jurisdictions. Recent years have witnessed a spate of litigation particularly in North America where family members have protested, on religious grounds, against the termination of respiratory and other life-sustaining support from patients who have been diagnosed dead using neurological criteria.[86] Of these, the most high profile is the case of Jahi McMath[87] whom after being declared brain dead, hence dead, under California's Uniform Determination of Death Act, was moved to New Jersey following an arduous legal battle by her family. Whilst New Jersey recognises whole brain death as a legal standard for

[77] Apart from the USA, these include Australia, Belgium, Malaysia, New Zealand and Turkey. See Australian and New Zealand Intensive Care Society (2021); Robbins and Bernat (2018) at 270; Malaysian Medical Council (2006), p. 8; Turkish Neurological Society Diagnostic Guidelines for Brain Death.

[78] E.g. Colombia, Cyprus, Greece, India, Malta, Poland, Trinidad and Tobago, Uruguay—see Lewis et al. (2020) at e301.

[79] See discussion in Chap. 4.

[80] Wijdicks (2006) at 540; Settergren (2003) at 1053.

[81] S.E. Gross, S. Lavi and H. Boas, op. cit., pp. 190–191; Truog (2020) at S76.

[82] Nair-Collins and Miller (2017) at 747–750; Carpenter and Reddi (2013), p. 292; Manzei (2016), p. 134; Doran and Vukov (2019) at 293.

[83] Lock (2004) at 135.

[84] Airedale NHS Trust v. Bland [1993] AC 789, per Lord Browne-Wilkinson at 878.

[85] Lundin (2012), pp. 27–28; Kerstis and Widarsson (2020) at pp. 3 and 10.

[86] E.g. *Fonseca v. Kaiser Permanent Medical Center Roseville and Others*, Case No. 2:16-CV-60889-KJM-EFB (2016); *Ouanounou v. Humber River Hospital et al.* 2017 ONSC 6511; *Nakar v. New York Presbyterian Hospital, Columbia University Irving Medical Center, and Milstein Pavilion Medical Intensive Care Unit*, No. 1780/2017 (Kings County Supreme Court, NY, 2019); *McKitty v. Hayani*, 2019 ONCA 805.

[87] *Winkfield v. Children's Hospital and Research Center at Oakland, California Northern District Court Oakland Division*, Case No. C 13–05,993 (2013).

declaring death, the state's Declaration of Death Act 1991 provides an exemption to accommodate personal religious beliefs. Section 5 of the Act states that the death of an individual shall not be declared upon the basis of neurological criteria when such a declaration would violate the individual's personal religious beliefs. In these circumstances, death should instead be declared on the basis of cardio-respiratory criteria. McMath's case has emboldened other families to translate their concerns into legal claims.[88] Importantly, this trend is observable not only in North America, but also in the UK.[89]

The ensuing chapters will explore the development of DNC in the UK from medical and legal perspectives.

References

Ackerknecht, E.H. 1968. Death in the History of Medicine. *Bulletin of the History of Medicine* 42 (1): 19–23.

Ad Hoc Committee of the Harvard Medical School to Examine the Definition of Brain Death. 1968. A Definition of Irreversible Coma. *Journal of the American Medical Association* 205 (6): 85–88

Agamben, G. 2017. *The Omnibus Homo Sacer*. Stanford: Stanford University Press.

American Academy of Orthopaedic Surgeons. 2005. *Emergency Care and Transportation of the Sick and Injured*. Massachusetts: Jones and Bartlett Publishers.

Anandaciva, S. 2020. Critical Care Services in the English NHS. *The King's Fund*, November 25.

Australian and New Zealand Intensive Care Society. 2021. The Statement on Death and Organ Donation (Melbourne: edition 4.1).

Brown, B., and J. Roberts. 2019. Principles of Artificial Ventilation. *Anaesthesia and Intensive Care Medicine* 20 (2): 72–84.

Capron, A.M. 2018. Beecher Dépassé: Fifty Years of Determining Death, Legally. *Hastings Center Report* 48 (6): S14–S18.

Carpenter, R., and B. Reddi. 2013. *Neurophysiology: A Conceptual Approach*. Boca Raton: CRC Press.

Converse, R. 1975. But When Did He Die? Tucker v Lower and the Brain-Death Concept. *San Diego Law Review* 12 (2): 424–435.

Corrado, A., and M. Gorini. 2002. Negative Pressure Ventilation: Is There Still A Role? *European Respiratory Journal* 20: 187–197.

Crawford, A.Z., et al. 2013. A Brief History of Corneal Transplantation: From Ancient to Modern. *Oman Journal of Opthalmology* 6 (Suppl 1): S12–S17.

Daniel, C. 1997. *Death and Burial in Medieval England 1066–1550*. London: Routledge.

Devettere, R.J. 2010. *Practical Decision-Making in Health Care Ethics: Cases and Concepts*. Washington: Georgetown University Press.

Doran, S.E., and J.M. Vukov. 2019. Organ Donation and Declaration of Death: Combined Neurologic and Cardiopulmonary Standards. *The Linacre Quarterly* 86 (4): 285–296.

Ervin, J.E., et al. 2018. Teamwork in the Intensive Care Unit. *American Psychologist* 73 (4): 468–477.

Evans, D.W. 2000. The Demise of "Brain Death" in Britain. In Beyond Brain Death: The Case Against Brain Based Criteria for Human Death, eds. M. Potts, P.A. Byrne and R.G. Nilges, 139–158. Dordrecht: Kluwer Academic Publishers.

[88] Pope (2018) at S46.

[89] See discussion in Chap. 3.

Gardiner, D., et al. 2012. International Perspective on the Diagnosis of Death. *British Journal of Anaesthesia* 108 (Supplement 1): i14–i28.
Gilder, S.S.B. 1968. Twenty-Second World Medical Assembly. *British Medical Journal* 3: 493–494.
Greer, D.M. 2020. Determination of Brain Death/Death by Neurologic Criteria: The World Brain Death Project. *Journal of the American Medical Association* 324 (11): 1078–1097.
Gross, S.E., S. Lavi, and H. Boas. 2019. Medicine, Technology and Religion Reconsidered: The Case of Brain Death Definition in Israel. *Science, Technology and Human Values* 44 (2): 186–208.
Hamilton, D. 2012. *A History of Organ Transplantation: Ancient Legends to Modern Practice*. Pittsburgh: University of Pittsburgh Press.
Hayman, J., and M. Oxenham. 2016. *Human Body Decomposition*. London: Academic Press.
Hutchison, E.D. 2008. *Dimensions of Human Behavior: The Changing Life Course*. California: Sage Publications Inc.
Ibsen, B. 1954. The Anaesthetist's Viewpoint on the Treatment of Respiratory Complications in Poliomyelitis During the Epidemic in Copenhagen, 1952. *Proceedings of the Royal Society of Medicine* 47 (1): 72–74.
Johnson, L.S.M. 2016. The Case for Reasonable Accommodation of Conscientious Objections to Declarations of Brain Death. *Bioethical Inquiry* 13: 105–115.
Johnson, L.S.M. 2017. Death by Neurological Criteria: Expert Definitions and Lay Misgivings. *QJM: an International Journal of Medicine* 110 (5): 267–270.
Jonsen, A.R. 1998. *The Birth of Bioethics*. New York: Oxford University Press.
Jonsen, A.R. 2012. The Ethics of Organ Transplantation: A Brief History. *Virtual Mentor* 14 (3): 264–268.
Kalitzkus, V. 2004. Neither Dead-nor-Alive: Organ Donation and the Paradox of "Living Corpses". In *Making Sense of Dying and Death*, ed. A. Fagan, 141–156. Amsterdam: Rodopi B.V.
Kelly, F.E., et al. 2014. Intensive Care Medicine is 60 Years Old: The History and Future of the Intensive Care Unit. *Clinical Medicine* 14 (4): 376–379.
Kerridge, I.H., et al. 2002. Death, Dying and Donation: Organ Transplantation and the Diagnosis of Death. *Journal of Medical Ethics* 28: 89–94.
Kerstis, B., and M. Widarsson. 2020. When Life Ceases—Relatives' Experiences When a Family Member Is Confirmed Brain Dead and Becomes a Potential Organ Donor—A Literature Review. *SAGE Open Nursing* 6: 1–15.
Lassen, H.C.A. 1954. The Epidemic of Poliomyelitis in Copenhagen, 1952. *Proceedings of the Royal Society of Medicine* 47 (1): 67–71.
Laureys, S., and J.J. Fins. 2008. Are We Equal in Death? Avoiding Diagnostic Error in Brain Death. *Neurology* 70: e14–e15.
Lawrence, J.J. 1893. The Diaphanous Test of Death. *The Medical Brief—A Monthly Journal of Practical Medicine* XXI (7): 1250.
Lewis, A., et al. 2020. Determination of Death by Neurologic Criteria Around the World. *Neurology* 95: e299–e309.
Lichtenstein, D. 2014. Ten Good Reasons to Practice Ultrasound in Critical Care. *Anaesthesiology Intensive Therapy* 46 (5): 323–335.
Lock, M. 2004. Living Cadavers and the Calculation of Death. *Body and Society* 10 (2–3): 135–152.
Lundin, S. 2012. Moral Accounting: Ethics and Praxis in Biomedical Research. In *The Atomized Body: The Cultural Life of Stem Cells, Genes and Neurons*, eds. M. Liljefors et al. Lund: Nordic Academic Press.
Machado, C. 2007. *Brain Death: A Reappraisal*. New York: Springer.
Machado, C., et al. 2007. The Declaration of Sydney on Human Death. *Journal of Medical Ethics* 33 (12): 699–703.
MacIntyre, N., C. Rackley, and F. Khusid. 2021. Fifty Years of Mechanical Ventilation—1970s to 2020. *Critical Care Medicine* 49 (4): 558–574.
Malaysian Medical Council. 2006. Brain Death. MMC Guideline 008/2006.

Mant, A.K. 1987. Knowledge Acquired from Post-War Exhumations. In *Death, Decay and Reconstruction: Approaches to Archaeology and Forensic Science*, eds. A. Bodkington et al. Manchester: Manchester University Press.

Manzei, A. 2016. Organ Shortage as a Structural Problem in Transplantation Medicine. In *Organ Transplantation in Times of Donor Shortage: Challenges and Solutions*, eds. R.J. Jox et al. New York: Springer.

Marshall, J.C., et al. 2017. What is an Intensive Care Unit? A Report of the Task Force of the World Federation of Societies of Intensive and Critical Care Medicine. *Journal of Critical Care* 37: 270–276.

Miller, F.G., and R.D. Truog. 2012. *Death, Dying, and Organ Transplantation: Reconstructing Medical Ethics at the End of Life*. New York: Oxford University Press.

Mollaret, P., and M. Goulon. 1959. Le Coma Dépassé (Memoire Preliminaire). *Révue Neurologique* 101: 3–15.

Munoz R.T., and M.D. Fox. 2013. Legal Aspects of Brain Death and Organ Donorship. In *The Brain-Dead Organ Donor: Pathophysiology and Management*, eds. D. Novitzky and D.K.C. Cooper, 21–36. New York: Springer.

Nair-Collins, M., and F.G. Miller. 2017. Do the "Brain Dead" Merely Appear to be Alive? *Journal of Medical Ethics* 43: 747–753.

Nair-Collins, M. 2022. Expanding the Social Status of "Corpse" to the Severely Comatose: Henry Beecher and the Harvard Brain Death Committee. *Perspectives in Biology and Medicine* 65 (1): 41–58.

Nguyen, D. 2019a. "Brain Death", Organ Donation and Presumed Consent: Consent Cannot Be Presumed Because "Brain Death" is Not True Death. *Aemaet* 8 (1): 1–66.

Nguyen, D. 2019b. Evolution of the Criteria of "Brain Death". A Critical Analysis Based on Scientific Realism and Christian Anthropology. *The Linacre Quarterly* 86 (4): 297–313.

NHS. Intensive Care. Available at https://www.nhs.uk/conditions/intensive-care/.

Nipper, B. 2017. Legislating Death: A Review and Proposed Refinement of the Uniform Determination of Death. *Houston Journal of Health Law and Policy* 17: 429–462.

Nordham, K.D., and S. Ninokawa. 2022. The History of Organ Transplantation. *Baylor University Medical Center Proceedings* 35 (1): 124–128.

Pearson, I.Y. 1995. Brain Death and Organ Donation. *Anaesthesia and Intensive Care* 23 (1): 11–13.

Pincock, S. 2007. Bjørn Aage Ibsen. *The Lancet* 379: 1538.

Pontificia Academia Pro Vita Assembly. The Dignity of the Dying.

Pope, T. 2018. Brain Death and the Law: Hard Cases and Legal Challenges. *Hastings Center Report* 48 (6): S46–S48.

Pope, T.M. 2015. Brain Death Rejected: Expanding Legal Duties to Accommodate Religious Objections. Proceedings from the 2015 Annual Conference, Petrie-Flom Center for Health Policy, Biotechnology, and Bioethics, Harvard Law School. Available at SSRN: https://ssrn.com/abstract=2699983.

President's Commission for the Study of Ethical Problems in Medicine and Biomedical and Behavioral Research. 1981. *A Report on the Medical, Legal and Ethical Issues in the Determination of Death*. Washington: Government Printing Office.

President's Commission for the Study of Ethical Problems in Medicine and Biomedical and Behavioral Research. 1983. *Summing Up: Final Report on Studies on the Ethical and Legal Problems in Medicine and Biomedical and Behavioral Research*. Washington: Government Printing Office.

Prioreschi, P. 1996. *A History of Medicine Volume I Primitive and Ancient Medicine*. Omaha Horatius Press.

Robbins, N.M., and J.L. Bernat. 2018. When Do You Order Ancillary Tests to Determine Brain Death? *Neurology Clinical Practice* 8 (3): 266–274.

Robertson, J.A. 1999. The Dead Donor Rule. *Hastings Center Report* 29 (6): 6–14.

Romero-Ávila, P., C. Márquex-Espinos, and J.R. Cabrera-Afonso. 2020. The History of Mechanical Ventilation. *Revista Médica De Chile* 148: 822–830.

Sade, R.M. 2011. Brain Death, Cardiac Death, and the Dead Donor Rule. *Journal of South Carolina Medical Association* 107 (4): 146–149.

Sarbey, B. 2016. Definitions of Death: Brain Death and What Matters in a Person. *Journal of Law and the Biosciences* 743–752.

Schlich, T. 2011. The Origins of Organ Transplantation. *The Lancet* 378: 1372–1373.

Settergren, G. 2003. Brain Death: An Important Paradigm Shift in the 20th Century. *Anaesthesiologica Scandinavica* 47 (9): 1053–1058.

Sole, M.L., et al. 2021. *Introduction to Critical Care Nursing*. Missouri: Elsevier.

Stone, W.M. (ed.). 1872. *The Half Yearly Abstract of the Medical Sciences*, Vol. LVI.

Sturgis, C.C. 1942. The History of Blood Transfusion. *Bulletin of the Medical Library Association* 30 (2): 105–112.

Trubuhovich, R.V. 2003. In the Beginning. The 1952–1953 Danish Epidemic of Poliomyelitis and Bjørn Ibsen. *Critical Care and Resuscitation* 5 (3), 227–230.

Truog, R.D. 2020. Defining Death: Lessons From the Case of Jahi McMath. *Pediatrics* 146: S75–S80.

Turkish Neurological Society. Diagnostic Guidelines for Brain Death.

Veatch, R.M. 2018. Would a Reasonable Person Now Accept the 1968 Harvard Brain Death Report? A Short History of Brain Death. *Hastings Center Report* S6–S9.

Vincent, J. 2013. Critical Care – Where Have We Been and Where Are We Going? *Critical Care* 17 (Supplement 1): S2.

Watson, C.J.E., and J.H. Dark. 2012. Organ Transplantation: Historical Perspective and Current Practice. *British Journal of Anaesthesia* 108 (Suppl 1): i29–i42.

Weil, M.H., and W. Tang. 2011. From Intensive Care to Critical Care Medicine: A Historical Perspective. *American Journal of Respiratory and Critical Care Medicine* 183: 1451–1453.

Wertheim, B.M. 2020. How a Polio Outbreak in Copenhagen Led to the Invention of the Ventilator. *Covid-19: A Smithsonian Magazine Special Report*, June 10.

West, J.B. 2005. The Physiological Challenges of the 1952 Copenhagen Poliomyelitis Epidemic and A Renaissance in Clinical Respiratory Physiology. *Journal of Applied Physiology* 99 (2): 424–432.

Wijdicks, E.F.M. 2006. The Clinical Criteria of Brain Death Throughout the World: Why Has it Come to This? *Canadian Journal of Anesthesia* 53 (6): 540–543.

Wijdicks, E.F.M. 2013a. Brain Death. In *Ethical and Legal Issues in Neurology*, ed. J.L. Bernat and R. Beresford, 191–204. Amsterdam: Elsevier BV.

Wijdicks, E.F.M. 2013b. *Famous First Papers for the Neurointensivist*. New York: Springer.

Wijdicks, E.F.M. 2017. *Brain Death*. New York: Oxford University Press.

Wijdicks, E.F.M., et al. 2011. The Early Days of the Neurosciences Intensive Care Unit. *Mayo Clinic Proceedings* 86 (9): 903–906.

Woodruff, M.F.A. 1966. Transplantation: The Clinical Problem. In *Ethics in Medical Progress: With Special Reference to Transplantation*, eds. G.E.W. Wolstenholme and M. O'Connor, 6–23. Boston: Little, Brown & Co.

World Medical Association. About Us. Available at https://www.wma.net/who-we-are/about-us/.

Young, J.D., and M.K. Sykes. 1990. Artificial Ventilation: History, Equipment and Techniques. *Thorax* 45: 753–758.

Zhu, H. and G. Han. 2021. Introduction of Sudden Death. In *Sudden Death: Advances in Diagnosis and Treatment*, ed. H. Zhu. Singapore: Springer.

Chapter 2
The Emergence of Neurological Death in the UK

Abstract This chapter documents the historical evolution of death by neurological criteria (DNC) in the UK. It investigates the factors behind its emergence and discusses the various changes that took place in the last few decades that culminated in the current definition and criteria for determining brain-based death. The chapter ends by highlighting the continuities and discontinuities in practice, and the impact they have on the issue of withdrawal of mechanical ventilation in ICUs and on the field of organ transplantation.

Keywords Death by neurological criteria · Brain stem death · Academy of Medical Royal Colleges · Withdrawal of ventilation · Organ donation

2.1 Introduction

In British intensive care units (ICUs) and neurological centres, death is currently determined by reference to brain stem death. This chapter traces the historical evolution of death by neurological criteria (DNC) in the UK from a medical perspective. It investigates the driving force behind the development and discusses the various changes that took place in the last few decades that culminated in the current definition and criteria for determining neurological death in relation to adults and children, and for very young infants. The chapter ends by highlighting the continuities and discontinuities in practice, and their significance in relation to the use of mechanical ventilation in ICUs and to the field of organ transplantation.

2.2 Historical Development

Death by neurological criteria, as discussed in the previous chapter, emerged mainly as a response to challenges posed by the increasing use of mechanical ventilation within modern ICUs. This phenomenon in some parts of Europe and the USA,

K. A. Choong, *The Medico-Legal Development of Neurological Death in the UK*,
https://doi.org/10.1007/978-981-19-6763-4_2

was also taking place in the UK at around the same time.[1] Hence it was not long before a similar dilemma as regards the justifiability of continuous ventilation of deeply comatose and unresponsive patients who have sustained severe brain damage confronted the medical profession here. The Conference of Medical Royal Colleges and Their Faculties in the United Kingdom played a pivotal role in this matter. Established in 1976, this is the coordinating body for the UK and Ireland's Medical Royal Colleges and Faculties. It was renamed the Academy of Medical Royal Colleges in 1996.[2]

In 1976, the Conference issued a statement entitled 'Diagnosis of Brain Death'. Importantly, it claimed that: "permanent functional death of the brain stem constitutes brain death and that once this has occurred further artificial support is fruitless and should be withdrawn."[3] According to the report, before a diagnosis of brain death is considered, the following 3 conditions should co-exist: the patient is deeply comatose; the patient is being maintained on a ventilator as spontaneous respiration had previously become inadequate or had ceased altogether; and there should be no doubt that the patient's condition is due to irremediable structural brain damage. The diagnosis of a disorder which can lead to brain death should have been fully established.[4]

In confirming brain death, it was noted that all brain-stem reflexes should be absent. The following must be determined: the pupils are fixed in diameter and do not respond to sharp changes in the intensity of incident light; there is no corneal reflex; the vestibuloocular reflexes are absent; no motor responses within the cranial nerve distribution can be elicited by adequate stimulation of any somatic area; there is no gag reflex or reflex response to bronchial stimulation by a suction catheter passed down the trachea; no respiratory movements occur when the patient is disconnected from the mechanical ventilator for long enough to ensure that the arterial carbon dioxide tension rises above the threshold for stimulating respiration.[5]

The tests are to usually be repeated to minimise observer error, particularly for conditions where the outcome is not clear cut. Once the criteria above are fulfilled, a decision on the withdrawal of mechanical ventilation can be made either by: a consultant in charge of the case and one other doctor; or his deputy (who has been registered for at least 5 years and who should have had adequate experience on such cases) and one other doctor.[6]

Although the Conference was influenced and dependent on the *Ad Hoc* Committee of the Harvard Medical School's Report,[7] it did not equate brain death with the demise of the person. Rather, it considered a diagnosis of brain death as indicative of futility. Once this has dawned, the continuation of ventilation and LST was said to only be

---

[1] Conference of Medical Royal Colleges and Their Faculties in the United Kingdom (1976) at 1187.

[2] Academy of Medical Royal Colleges, 'Who We Are' at https://www.aomrc.org.uk/about-us/.

[3] Conference of Medical Royal Colleges and Their Faculties in the United Kingdom, op. cit., p. 1187.

[4] Ibid.

[5] Ibid., pp. 1187–1188.

[6] Ibid., p. 1188.

[7] Evans (2001) at 144.

providing families with "sterile hope".[8] Thus the criteria outlined were meant to separate those who had a chance of even partial recovery, from those with none. Ventilation and LST could be withdrawn from the latter on the grounds that the patient had no chance of recovery, not because they were already dead.[9] The link between brain death and organ donation, if any, was also not made explicit at this stage of DNC's history in the UK. It was discernible only through an acknowledgement that the diagnostic criteria were drafted with the assistance of the subcommittee of the Transplant Advisory Panel. Even so, the panel was only one of three advisory bodies.[10]

If the 1976 report never equated brain death with the death of the patient,[11] this took place three years later. In an Addendum issued in January 1979, the Conference published the decision it arrived at after examining the question of whether, upon the occurrence of brain death, death should be presumed.[12] Published under the title 'Diagnosis of Death', the Conference took the view that "[b]rain death represents the stage at which a patient becomes truly dead, because by then all functions of the brain have permanently and irreversibly ceased".[13] This is so, irrespective of whether "the function of some organ, such as a heartbeat, is still maintained by artificial means".[14] Hence, a shift was made from brain death as the yardstick by which the withdrawal of futile life-support could be justified, to it representing the stage at which a patient is viewed as having died.[15] No change was introduced to the diagnosis protocol. In other words, the very same criteria previously used for prognostic purposes were now used for the purpose of diagnosing death.[16]

It is necessary to highlight that the document contained two glaring omissions. One, that no explanation was provided for the massive leap in interpretation.[17] Two, that no direct reference was made as to whether this development was associated with organ transplantation. The former was eventually proffered in 1995 when the Conference endorsed a Review conducted by a Working Group convened by the Royal College of Physicians (RCP) on the then existing criteria used in the diagnosis of brain death. Before this is looked at, it is interesting to observe that the latter was strongly hinted at when the Health Departments of Great Britain and Northern Ireland published a *Code of Practice for the Removal of Cadaveric Organs for*

---

[8] Conference of Medical Royal Colleges and Their Faculties in the United Kingdom, op. cit., p. 1187.

[9] D.A. Jones, 'The UK Definition of Death', available at https://www.lifeissues.net/writers/jon/jon_01death.html.

[10] The other two were the Working Party of the Royal College of Physicians, and the Working Party of the Faculty of Anaesthetists and the Royal College of Surgeons.

[11] D.A. Jones, op. cit.

[12] Conference of Medical Royal Colleges and Their Faculties in the United Kingdom (1979).

[13] Ibid., paragraph 7.

[14] Ibid., paragraph 9.

[15] Not anticipating the legal challenges that were brought to court just over 3 decades later, the Conference added that "[i]t is not difficult or illogical in any way to equate this with the concept in many religions of the departure of the spirit from the body"—paragraph 7.

[16] D.W. Evans, op. cit., p. 145.

[17] D.A. Jones, op. cit.

Transplantation in October 1979, merely months after the Conference's Addendum was issued.[18] This was at the instigation of the Transplant Advisory Panel, which as mentioned above, was one of the advisory bodies to the Conference's 1976 statement. The Panel was concerned that the supply of cadaveric kidneys for transplantation was then only half of what was necessary to meet the demand. They attributed the shortfall partly to the hesitancy on the part of hospital staff to identify potential donors from among their dying patients, and to initiate the procedures leading to transplantation. They highlighted that there was also often uncertainty relating to what those procedures were, and that the factors affecting kidney supply were also adversely affecting the supply of eyes for corneal grafting.[19] The Code of Practice, which was prepared by a Working Party chaired by Lord Smith of Marlow, set out to be a model of basic guidelines for the use of staff of hospitals that may have potential organ donors as well as staff of hospitals which carry out organ transplantation. While its main focus was on kidney transplant, it was also applicable to other organs like hearts and livers, and made specific provisions for corneas.[20]

According to the Code, patients who may become suitable donors after death are those who have sustained severe and irreversible brain damage. They were dependent on artificial ventilation or expected to be so imminently.[21] Importantly, the Code endorsed and applied the position taken by the Conference that death could be diagnosed by the irreversible cessation of brain stem function ('brain death'). This is in addition to the traditional method of irreversible cessation of respiration and heartbeat.[22] To diagnose brain death, it emphasised that the criteria outlined by the Conference were to be followed.[23] For death determined in this manner, or where organs were to be removed within an hour after respiration and circulation have stopped, it stated that death should be diagnosed by a Consultant who is in charge of the case or his deputy, and one other doctor. None of the doctors should be a member of the transplant team.[24] The Code affirmed that "[i]t is ethical to maintain artificial ventilation and heart beat until the removal of organs has been completed. This is essential in the case of heart and liver transplants and many doctors think it is desirable when removing kidneys. The removal should always be carried out under normal operating theatre conditions and may proceed at any convenient time after the diagnosis of death."[25]

The Code therefore validated and reinforced the Conference's view that brain stem death equates the death of the person. Once brain stem death is confirmed, vital and non-vital organs could be removed from a body which is still ventilated and whose organs are still perfused with oxygenated blood. Thus not only could the so-called

---

[18] Health Departments of Great Britain and Northern Ireland (1979).

[19] Ibid., p. 5.

[20] Ibid., paragraph 38.

[21] Ibid., paragraph 5.

[22] Ibid., paragraph 27.

[23] Ibid.

[24] Ibid., paragraph 28.

[25] Ibid., paragraph 33.

"heartbeating donor"[26] be a source of multiple transplantable organs, those organs could also be removed while fully functional and in a condition which is optimal for transplantation.[27]

When the Code was updated in 1983[28] under the title of *Cadaveric Organs for Transplantation: A Code of Practice Including the Diagnosis of Brain Death*,[29] the association between neurological death and organ transplantation was strengthened and made more visible through the incorporation of the former in the title. The Code reiterated its support of the Conference's view that death can, in addition to the traditional cardio-respiratory criteria, be diagnosed by the irreversible cessation of brain stem function.[30] Further, in diagnosing brain death, the criteria outlined by the Conference should be complied with.[31] Through this, the Code authorised the removal of organs from heart-beating donors or the "living bodies".[32]

Returning to the aforementioned Review which the Conference endorsed in 1995,[33] this document aimed to update the 2 documents the Conference produced in 1976 and 1979, as well as the 1983 Code of Practice. The Review explained that death should be defined as the "irreversible loss of the capacity for consciousness, combined with irreversible loss of the capacity to breathe".[34] And since the irreversible cessation of brain stem function (brain stem death) will produce this clinical state, it emphasised that "brain stem death is equivalent to the death of the individual".[35] In view of this, it suggested that "the more correct" term of "brain stem death"[36] should replace "brain death", the term used thus far by the Conference and the Health Departments of Great Britain and Northern Ireland.[37] By providing a definition of death, the Review explained why brain stem death denotes the death of the patient. It was highlighted that upon a diagnosis of brain stem death, the hearts of ventilated patients will cease beating within a few days or at most, a few weeks.[38] There would still be movement of the limbs and torso after brain stem death, but

---

26 McKeown et al. (2012) at i96.

27 Wright (2007).

28 Between the 2 Codes, the British Broadcasting Corporation (BBC) aired 'Transplants: Are the Donors Really Dead?' (on 13 October 1980) and 'A Question of Life or Death: The Brain Death Debate' (on 19 February 1981), which had a strong impact on public confidence relating to DNC and organ transplant. For discussion, see Wijdicks (2012); Jennett et al. (1980).

29 Health Departments of Great Britain and Northern Ireland (1983).

30 Ibid., paragraph 28.

31 Ibid.

32 Evans (2012) at 16.

33 Working Group Convened by the Royal College of Physicians (1995).

34 Ibid., p. 381.

35 Ibid.

36 This corresponds to the view expressed by Pallis, who also sat in this Working Group, shortly after the release of the 1979 Addendum that "[i]f we accept the concept of brain stem death it might be wise to change the words we use and no longer speak of 'brain death' when we mean 'brain stem death'"—see Pallis (1982) at 1438.

37 Working Group Convened by the Royal College of Physicians op. cit., p. 381.

38 Ibid.

the Review stressed that these are of a reflex, rather than of a voluntary, nature.[39] Confirming the validity of the Conference's clinical criteria for diagnosis of brain stem death, the Review outlined the following as essential conditions which need to be satisfied before the diagnosis of brain stem death is considered or further investigated: there should be no doubt that the patient's condition is due to irremediable brain damage of known aetiology; the patient is deeply comatose; and the patient is mechanically ventilated because spontaneous respiration has become inadequate or has ceased completely.[40]

In 1998, *A Code of Practice for the Diagnosis of Brain Stem Death: Including Guidelines for the Identification and Management of Potential Organ and Tissue Donors* was issued by a Working Party established through the RCP. More than half of the membership of this Working Party sat on the Working Group which published the 1995 Review. This Code of Practice was produced on behalf of the Academy of Medical Royal Colleges (the new name for the Conference) at the request of the Department of Health.[41] Notably, the title made use of the new term "brain stem death" rather than "brain death". Contrasted to the 1983 Code of Practice, the order of neurological death and organ donation was reversed in the title. Hence the association between them was slightly softened by this revised Code of Practice.[42] The document incorporated the definition of death espoused by the 1995 Review, which is that it should be regarded as the irreversible loss of the capacity for consciousness, combined with irreversible loss of the capacity to breathe. It highlighted that the irreversible cessation of brain stem function would produce this clinical state.[43]

The Code began by emphasising that when the brain stem of a coma patient has been damaged in such a way and to such an extent that its functions are irreversibly destroyed, this condition is described as brain stem death.[44] The criteria for establishing this are as per those set out in the 1983 Code of Practice (i.e. by the Conference's 1976 document). Once these criteria are met, "the patient is dead"[45] and mechanical life-support can be withdrawn. It pointed out that it is also proper "to consider whether any of the dead patient's organs can be made available for transplant into another patient".[46] If so, the maintenance of normal homeostasis by attempting to ensure adequate fluid intake, electrolyte balance, normal blood pressure, the monitoring of urine output by catheter collection and the use of other therapeutic agents, which is usually part of the standard care of a patient whose brain stem has not been diagnosed dead, may be continued after confirmation of brain stem death so as to

39 Ibid.

40 Ibid., p. 382.

41 Department of Health (1998).

42 Price (2000) p. 44.

43 Department of Health, op. cit., p. 3.

44 Ibid., p. 1.

45 Ibid.

46 Ibid.

preserve the condition of the organs to be donated.[47] The document also contained detailed guidelines on the sequence of events from diagnosis of brain stem death leading to organ or tissue donation.

2.3 Current Guidelines

The Academy of Medical Royal Colleges has since published an updated *Code of Practice for the Diagnosis and Confirmation of Death* in 2008. As this Code of Practice and the Conference's reports which preceded it relate to the criteria to be fulfilled before withdrawing ventilation and LST from comatose adults, they are, and have been, used in adult ICUs and neurological centres. However, as sophisticated intensive care can likewise be offered to infants, a similar question of when to withdraw ventilation from infants whose brains are irreversibly damaged inevitably arose. The Royal College of Paediatrics and Child Heath (RCPCH), previously known as the British Paediatric Association (BPA), has recommended that the criteria used to establish death for children over 2 months old should be the same as those used for adults. In relation to those who are 2 months old or less, the recommendations made by the RCPCH in 2015 are now followed. The Academy's Code of Practice and the RCPCH's recommendations are the current guidelines in use. These will be looked at in turn.

2.3.1 Adults and Children Over 2 Months Old

Writing in the Foreword of the Academy's 2008 Code of Practice, the then Chief Medical Officer Sir Liam Donaldson conveyed his confidence that the Code "provides clear, scientifically rigorous criteria for confirming death, both in clinical settings where confirmation of death by brain stem testing is appropriate, and where confirmation of death following cardiac arrest is required."[48] The Code of Practice aimed to spare family, friends and carers the ordeal of witnessing prolonged interventions which are not in the patients' best interests.[49] Likewise, it serves to ensure that healthcare professionals involved in this area of medicine can feel confident about the acceptability of interventions which were said to merely prolong somatic function.[50]

According to the document, death involves the permanent loss of those features that are vital and indispensable to the survival of a living human being. Endorsing the views of its predecessor, it stated that the definition of death should be considered as "the irreversible loss of the capacity for consciousness, combined with irreversible

47 Ibid., p. 8.

48 Academy of Medical Royal Colleges (2008), p. 5.

49 Ibid., p. 7.

50 Ibid.

loss of the capacity to breathe".[51] It added that since the irreversible cessation of brain stem function will bring about this clinical state, the "irreversible cessation of the integrative function of the brain stem equates with the death of the individual and allows the medical practitioner to diagnose death".[52] As with the Academy's earlier documents, three points were highlighted in relation to this. One, that those patients are no longer able to breathe unaided without ventilatory support (without which their lungs and heart are not carrying out their natural functions) as well as other life-sustaining interventions. This loss of function is irreversible and permanent. Secondly, this state does not entail the cessation of all neurological activity in the brain, but any potential activities are not indicative of any form of consciousness linked with human life and would not last for long in any event. Thirdly, some residual reflex movement of the limbs may be present, but this is controlled through the spinal cord rather than the brain. Thus whilst some parts of the body may still show signs of biological activity, it was stressed that these have no moral relevance to the declaration of death for the purpose of the immediate withdrawal of all supportive interventions.[53]

All of the following conditions must be satisfied before a diagnosis of death using neurological criteria can be undertaken: that the patient's condition is undoubtedly due to irreversible brain damage of known aetiology; the patient is deeply comatose, unresponsive and apnoeic, with his/her lungs being artificially ventilated; and the patient is maintained on ventilatory support because spontaneous respiration has ceased.

The Code of Practice recapitulated and thereby confirmed the guidelines outlined in the Conference's earlier documents relating to the criteria for the diagnosis of death following irreversible cessation of brain stem function. To ensure that brain stem reflexes are absent, the following must be ascertained: the pupils are fixed in diameter and do not respond to sharp changes in the intensity of incident light; there is no corneal reflex; the ocular-vestibular reflexes are absent; no motor responses within the cranial nerve distribution can be elicited by adequate stimulation of any somatic area; there is no cough reflex response to bronchial stimulation by a suction catheter placed down the trachea to the carina, or gag response to stimulation of the posterior pharynx with a spatula; and the process for testing the respiratory response to hypercarbia (apnoea test) should be the last brain stem reflex to be tested and should not be performed if any of the preceding tests confirm the presence of brain stem reflexes.[54]

Brain-stem testing to diagnose death must be performed twice.[55] They should be conducted by at least 2 medical practitioners who have been registered for more than 5 years. One of them, at least, must be a Consultant. They must all be competent in the conduct and interpretation of brain-stem testing. However, none of them should

---

[51] Ibid., p. 11.

[52] Ibid.

[53] Ibid.

[54] Ibid., p. 17.

[55] Ibid., p. 19.

be a member of the transplant team. The tests should be performed by the doctors acting together and a complete set of tests should be carried out on 2 occasions. Death is confirmed upon the conclusion of the second test.

The Code of Practice noted that even if artificial ventilation and cardiovascular support are maintained after death has been certified following cessation of brain stem reflexes, the patient's heart will ultimately stop beating. Although this usually happens within a few days, it can take weeks or even months if aggressive support is sustained. It is also common for endocrine, metabolic and circulatory abnormalities to appear in patients who suffer irreversible cessation of brain stem function following anoxic, haemorrhagic or traumatic cerebral injury. Further, reflex movements of the limbs and torso may still be observed, but these are of spinal-reflex origin and do not represent the higher functioning of the brain.[56]

This updated Code was produced after wide consultations including through networks supplied by the Human Tissue Authority (HTA) and UK Transplant.[57] Interestingly, it made a conscious and deliberate effort to decouple the diagnosis and confirmation of death from organ donation and transplantation. This was to presumably ward off criticism that the diagnosis of brain stem death is inextricably linked to the desire to obtain organs for transplantation. "The fact is", according to the Academy, "there is no logical relationship between them"[58] and "[a] definition of human death should not be related to organ transplantation".[59] Thus, unlike earlier Codes of Practice, organ transplantation was removed from its title and contents. Instead, it advised that this Code should be used in conjunction with the latest guidelines on organ donation and transplantation from the Intensive Care Society and the Codes of Practice from the HTA.

2.3.2 *Infants from 37 Weeks Corrected Gestation (Post Menstrual) to Two Months (Post Term) Old*

In 2015, at the request of the Academy, the RCPCH reviewed its position on the diagnosis of death using neurological criteria for infants under 2 months old. In 1991, it had produced *Diagnosis of Brain-Stem Death in Infants and Children: A Working Party Report of the British Paediatric Association*. The Report made recommendations relating to infants and children who are comatose, totally apnoeic and being ventilated, in which it recommended that the criteria used to determine death for children over 2 months old should be the same as for those used for adults. As regards those between 37 weeks of gestation and 2 months old, it took the view that it is rarely possible to confidently diagnose brain stem death.[60] As for those below

---

[56] Ibid., p. 19.

[57] Ibid., p. 7.

[58] Ibid.

[59] Ibid.

[60] British Paediatric Association (1991), paragraph 2.

37 weeks of gestation, the concept of brain stem death is considered inappropriate and the criteria for establishing it cannot therefore be applied.[61] Having reviewed the medical literature from 1990 to 2014 concerning the experience of other countries which do apply DNC in young infants in the presence of persisting cardiac function, the organisation revised its recommendations for infants from 37 weeks corrected gestation (post menstrual) to two months (post term) old.

The RCPCH published *The Diagnosis of Death by Neurological Criteria in Infants Less Than Two Months Old: Updated Recommendations* in 2015. This document recommended that the preconditions outlined in the 2008 Code of Practice should be satisfied before diagnosing brain stem death, namely that the patient is comatose and artificially ventilated for apnoea; and the diagnosis of structural brain damage has been made or the immediate cause of coma is known.[62] An additional precondition was deemed appropriate: in post-asphyxiated infants or those who received intensive care after resuscitation, there should at least be 24 h of observation during which the preconditions crucial for assessment for DNC should be present before clinical testing is conducted for DNC. The period of observation may be extended in situations where there are concerns relating to residual drug-induced sedation.[63]

The criteria for diagnosing death by neurological criteria outlined in the 2008 Code of Practice can likewise be used for infants in this specified age group absent brain stem reflexes; absent motor responses and no respiratory response to hypercarbia. However, it stated that the following precautionary measures should be considered for the apnoea test: the use of a stronger hypercarbic stimulus in order to establish respiratory unresponsiveness. Ancillary tests are not required for this age group.[64]

The report supports the repetition of testing and the rationale proffered by the Academy for this, which was to minimise the possibility of an incorrect diagnosis in case of error in the first examination. It did not recommend a precise interval between the 2 tests, but confirmed that it need not be prolonged as noted in the 2008 Code.[65] As for who should conduct the tests, this must be made by 2 paediatricians who have been registered for more than 5 years and are competent in the procedure. One of them should be a Consultant. They should undertake the testings together. These must always be carried out completely and successfully on 2 occasions in total.[66] The 2015 Report does not make recommendations for pre-term infants less than 37 weeks corrected gestation (post menstrual) age. Nor does it, just like the 2008 Code of Practice, cover issues surrounding organ donation and transplantation.

Satisfaction of the relevant brain stem death criteria outlined by the Academy of Medical Royal Colleges and the RCPCH means that doctors no longer have a duty to continue treating the brain stem dead patient. Withdrawal of ventilation and life-sustaining treatment would then be clinically justified and even indicated. When

---

[61] Ibid., paragraph 3.

[62] Royal College of Paediatrics and Child Health (2015), p. 18.

[63] Ibid.

[64] Ibid., p. 4.

[65] Ibid., p. 18.

[66] Ibid., p. 19.

read in conjunction with documents produced by the Intensive Care Society[67] and the HTA,[68] vital organs could also be removed from the ventilated bodies of brain stem dead patients who are identified as suitable and eligible donors.

2.4 Conclusion

In the UK, as elsewhere in Europe and the USA, determination of death by neurological criteria owed its provenance to the quest for an ethically defensible response on how to deal with deeply comatose and unresponsive patients on mechanical ventilation. In 1976, the Conference of Medical Royal Colleges and Their Faculties in the United Kingdom published a statement declaring that mechanical ventilation can be withdrawn from such patients as they have suffered permanent functional death of the brain stem. This state, according to the Conference, constituted brain death. Cessation of life-support, at this stage of DNC's history, was deemed justified on the grounds that further ventilation was futile. The patient was still alive rather than dead when this was removed. However, as discussed, this outlook was short-lived.

Just 3 years later in 1979, brain death was equated with the death of the human being itself. This recognition that death can be diagnosed using brain-based criteria survived to the present day. However, this is under the new term of "brain stem death" which was introduced in 1995. Notwithstanding these monumental changes, the pre-requisites, the diagnostic criteria, the number of tests to be conducted, and who are eligible to perform those tests have remained largely similar since 1976. When artificial ventilation is stopped, its withdrawal is now from a patient who is already dead. This is because they have suffered "irreversible loss of the capacity for consciousness, combined with irreversible loss of the capacity to breathe", namely a clinical state defined as death and which is produced by the irreversible cessation of brain stem function (i.e. brain stem death). If the patient is a suitable organ donor, their vital organs can be removed while they are still ventilated. This does not contravene the dead donor rule, as those patients are no longer considered alive.

However, the association between the new clinical definition of death and organ transplantation has not always been made clear nor consistent. A strong link was discernible in 1979 when a Code of Practice was released endorsing neurological death and confirming that it could be used for the purposes of heart-beating donation. Although this link was retained by the next few versions of the Code, efforts were made to gradually downplay any perceived connection. The latest iteration, the 2008 Code of Practice, even went as far as to remove organ transplantation from its title and contents. Denying and rejecting any relationship between DNC and organ transplantation, it advised that existing guidelines on organ donation and transplantation issued by specified organisations should instead be used in conjunction with the Code.

[67] E.g. Intensive Care Society (2021).

[68] E.g. Human Tissue Authority (2020), paragraph 56.

Throughout, cardio-respiratory criteria remained as a way to determine death. In other words, brain stem death did not subsume nor replace this traditional method of defining and diagnosing death. However, when it comes to the removal of ventilation in ICUs, this is the dominant definition of death.[69] This is both in the context of its removal for the purpose of handing the patient's body to the family for burial and cremation; and in the context of heart-beating organ donation.

The development of DNC in the UK is therefore marked by continuities and discontinuities. Further, despite being influenced and inspired by the Harvard *Ad Hoc* Committee's report, the path taken here was noticeably different. Spearheaded by professional bodies like the Academy of Medical Royal Colleges and the Royal College of Physicians, as well as the Department of Health, DNC began life within the framework of medical futility. The UK also focuses on a more specific part of the brain (namely the brain stem) compared to the USA's adoption of whole brain death as the indicator of neurological death. Further, unlike the USA, there is no statutory definition of death in the UK. Instead, as will be illustrated in the next chapter, DNC gained its legitimacy through case law.

References

Academy of Medical Royal Colleges. 2008. A Code of Practice for the Diagnosis and Confirmation of Death.

Academy of Medical Royal Colleges. Who We Are. at https://www.aomrc.org.uk/about-us/.

British Paediatric Association. 1991. Diagnosis of Brain-Stem Death in Infants and Children: A Working Party Report of the British Paediatric Association.

Conference of Medical Royal Colleges and Their Faculties in the United Kingdom. 1976. Diagnosis of Death: Statement Issued by the Honorary Secretary of the Conference of Medical Royal Colleges and their Faculties in the United Kingdom on 11 October 1976. *British Medical Journal* 2: 1187–1188.

Conference of Medical Royal Colleges and Their Faculties in the United Kingdom. 1979. Diagnosis of Death: Memorandum Issued by the Honorary Secretary of the Conference of Medical Royal Colleges and Their Faculties in the United Kingdom on 15 January 1979. *British Medical Journal* 1: 332.

Controversies in the Determination of Death. White Paper by the President's Council on Bioethics, Washington, 65–66.

Department of Health. 1998. A Code of Practice for the Diagnosis of Brain Stem Death: Including Guidelines for the Identification and Management of Potential Organ and Tissue Donors.

Evans, D. 2012. Brain Stem Death and Organ Transplantation. *Catholic Medical Quarterly* 62 (2): 15–20.

Evans, D.W. 2001. The Demise of "Brain Death" in Britain. In *Beyond Brain Death: The Case Against Brain Based Criteria for Human Death*, ed. M. Potts, P.A. Byrne, and R.G. Nilges, 139–158. Dordrecht: Kluwer Academic Publishers.

Health Departments of Great Britain and Northern Ireland. (1983). Cadaveric Organs for Transplantation: A Code of Practice Including the Diagnosis of Brain Death.

---

[69] As to be discussed in the next chapter, this seems to be the only one recognised by the courts for the clinical context.

Health Departments of Great Britain and Northern Ireland. 1979. The Removal of Cadaveric Organs for Transplantation: A Code of Practice.
Human Tissue Authority. 2020. Code F Donation of Solid Organs and Tissue for Transplantation (Part 2: Deceased Organ and Tissue Donation).
Intensive Care Society. 2021. Form for the Diagnosis of Death Using Neurological Criteria.
Jennett, B., et al. 1980. Transplants: Are the Donors Really Dead? *British Medical Journal* 281: 1139–1141.
Jones, D.A. The UK Definition of Death. Available at https://www.lifeissues.net/writers/jon/jon_01death.html.
McKeown, D.W., et al. 2012. Management of the Heartbeating Brain-Dead Organ Donor. *British Journal of Anaesthesia* 108 (S1): i96–i107.
Pallis, C. 1982. From Brain Death to Brain Stem Death. *British Medical Journal* 1487–1490.
Price, D. 2000. *Legal and Ethical Aspects of Organ Transplantation*. Cambridge: Cambridge University Press.
Royal College of Paediatrics and Child Health. 2015. The Diagnosis of Death by Neurological Criteria in Infants Less than Two Months Old.
Wijdicks, E.F.M. 2012. The Transatlantic Divide Over Brain Death Determination and the Debate *Brain* 135: 1321–1331.
Working Group Convened by the Royal College of Physicians. 1995. Criteria for the Diagnosis of Brain Stem Death: Review by a Working Group Convened by the Royal College of Physicians and Endorsed by the Conference of Medical Royal Colleges and their Faculties in the United Kingdom. *Journal of the Royal College of Physicians of London* 29 (5): 381–382.
Wright, D.W. 2007. Seeking an Ethical and Legal Way of Procuring Transplantable Organs From The Dying Without Further Attempts to Redefine Human Death. *Philosophy, Ethics, and Humanities in Medicine* 2. https://doi.org/10.1186/1747-5341-2-11.

Chapter 3
Death in the Courtroom

Abstract This chapter discusses the law's response to the introduction and development of death by neurological criteria in clinical practice. It will demonstrate how the legitimacy of the definition and criteria used by the medical profession was forged in the courtroom rather than Parliamentary chambers. It will explore why case law were introduced in court, and assesses whether organ donation was a consideration in the deliberations. The chapter ends by drawing attention to the trends and tendencies that have emerged over time.

Keywords Courts · Judges · Brain stem death · Case law · Code of Practice for the Diagnosis and Confirmation of Death · Withdrawal of ventilation · Religious objections

3.1 Introduction

Diagnosis of death using neurological criteria (DNC) has been the clinical method for defining death in British ICUs for nearly five decades. This chapter looks at the manner in which the law responds to this definition of death across this time span. It will demonstrate that the legitimacy of this definition and the criteria used by the medical profession was forged in the courtroom rather than Parliamentary chambers. It will explore why case law, whilst numerically small and relatively low profile[1] were introduced in court. It will also assess whether organ donation was a consideration in the deliberations. The chapter ends by drawing attention to the trends and tendencies that have emerged over the duration.

3.2 Judicial Endorsement of Neurological Death

The dilemmas thrust by artificial ventilation and modern ICU technology have given rise to a number of cases which were brought before the courts for resolution. Brain

[1] Especially when compared to end-of-life cases relating to physician-assisted death and medical futility in paediatrics.

K. A. Choong, *The Medico-Legal Development of Neurological Death in the UK*,
https://doi.org/10.1007/978-981-19-6763-4_3

stem death also received a mention in a number of cases when these were not the matters in contention. What do the courts' treatment of these cases demonstrate and imply? And how far does organ transplantation play a part in their deliberations? These are the main issues considered in this section.

3.2.1 From Brain Death to Brain Stem Death

The starting point for this part of the discussion is the 1981 jointly-heard cases of *R v. Richard Tadeusz Malcherek* and *R v. Anthony Steel.*[2] Frequently credited as the courts' first encounter with neurological death post the declarations made by the Conference of the Medical Royal Colleges,[3] it should be noted that the term 'brain death' was used by the judiciary in line with the terminology used in medicine at the time. These two unconnected cases were heard together in the Court of Appeal owing to their highly similar facts and proximity in time.

By way of background, Richard Malcherek had stabbed his wife multiple times with a kitchen knife leading her to suffer a massive haemorrhage. She was taken to Poole General Hospital, but transferred a few days later to the Western Hospital at Southampton. Meanwhile Anthony Steel savagely attacked and battered a woman about her head with a 50 lb stone, leading her to suffer multiple fractures of the skull and severe brain damage. She was found unconscious and taken to the Bradford Royal Infirmary. Both women were connected to ventilators upon their arrival at the respective hospitals. When medical teams determined that brain death had occurred, the ventilators were disconnected, asserting that the machines were merely operating on a lifeless body. Richard Malcherek and Anthony Steel were each charged with murder. Although they had submitted that the disconnection from ventilation broke the chain of causation, the Crown Court overruled this submission and withdrew the issue of causation from the jury. Both men were found guilty of murder. Malcherek was sentenced to life imprisonment by the Crown Court at Winchester. Steel was sentenced to life imprisonment by the Crown Court at Leeds. The trial judges held that there was evidence to suggest that after ventilatory support was removed, the

---

[2] (1981) 73 Cr. App. R. 173.

[3] There was nevertheless an interesting report in The Times on the outcome of an inquest relating to a John David Potter. After sustaining severe head injuries caused by a man called Henry Hall, Potter was admitted into hospital. 14 h after admission into hospital, he stopped breathing and was thereafter kept 24 h on artificial ventilation so that one of his kidneys could be taken for transplantation into another person. According to his doctor, when he ceased breathing, he had virtually died (although he noted that from a legal point of view, it would be more accurate to say that Potter died when his heart and circulation stopped). Consent for the removal seemed to have been obtained from his wife. After the removal of the kidney, the ventilator was switched off, and no spontaneous breathing or circulation were recorded. When the issue of whether the removal of the kidney led to his death was put before the jury, it seemed that they came to a decision that the act bore no connection to his death. Rather, they accepted that his death was caused by the initial brain injuries and found a manslaughter verdict against Hall for causing the death of Potter. See Anonymous (1963).

original wound or injury was a continuing, operating and substantial cause of both women's deaths.

As their appeals raised similar points, they were heard together in the Court of Appeal. Malcherek appealed against his conviction whilst Steel applied for leave to appeal against conviction. They *inter alia* contended that the trial judge in each case should have allowed the jury to decide on the issue of causation. They claimed that the doctors, by switching off the ventilation, were instead the cause of death and the jury should have been allowed to consider whether this was indeed the case. They also applied for leave to adduce further medical evidence to demonstrate that the 2 medical teams had not complied with all the Conference of Medical Royal Colleges' suggested criteria for establishing brain death and that these criteria were not sufficiently stringent. It was argued in *Steel* that two of the suggested tests, namely the corneal reflex test and the vestibular-ocular reflex test, had not been conducted properly.[4] In *Malcherek*, it was claimed that only 5 out of the 6 confirmatory tests were performed, and the gag reflex test was omitted.[5] In both cases, the medical teams provided explanations as to why those tests were not performed.

The appeal was dismissed, but without considering whether brain death was indeed death. "[T]his is not the occasion", the Court of Appeal pointed out, "for any decision as to what constitutes death".[6] Instead, the court drew attention to the fact that the question posed for them to answer was simply whether the Crown Court judges in both cases were right to withdraw the question of causation from the jury. In other words, were those judges right to find that there was no evidence on which the jury could come to the conclusion that the two men did not cause the death of the victims?[7] On this, the Court of Appeal stressed that: "[w]here a medical practitioner adopting methods which are generally accepted comes *bona fide* and conscientiously to the conclusion that the patient is for practical purposes dead, and that such vital functions as exist—for example, circulation—are being maintained solely by mechanical means, and therefore discontinues treatment, that does not prevent the person who inflicted the initial injury from being responsible for the victim's death".[8] As the cessation of artificial ventilation did not break the chain of causation between their action and the victims' deaths, the 2 men were not exonerated from murder. As if anticipating that the matter could come up again in the future, the Court added that it was "perhaps bizarre to suggest…that where a doctor tries his conscientious best to save the life of a patient brought to hospital *in extremis*, skilfully using sophisticated methods, drugs and machinery to do so, but fails in his attempt and therefore discontinues treatment, he can be said to have caused the death of the patient".[9] The Court also emphasised that it was no part of their task "to inquire whether the criteria, the Royal Medical College confirmatory tests, are a satisfactory

[4] At p. 177.

[5] At p. 178.

[6] At p. 179.

[7] At p. 179.

[8] At pp. 181–182.

[9] At p. 182.

code of practice", nor was it "to decide whether the doctors were, in either of these two cases, justified in omitting one or more of the so called 'confirmatory tests'. The doctors are not on trial."[10] The court refused to allow evidence to be submitted to show that other medical practitioners would have administered the treatment by a life support machine differently.

In endorsing the Conference's definition and criteria, the Court of Appeal therefore conferred legitimacy onto brain death as legal death. It follows that ventilation could be withdrawn from brain dead patients on the basis that they were already dead. The court also seemed to take a lenient or unquestioning stance when doctors did not carry out all the confirmatory tests outlined. By extension, even if not in their contemplation at the time, the Court of Appeal conferred legitimacy to heart-beating donation as advanced by the 1979 *Code of Practice for the Removal of Cadaveric Organs for Transplantation*, as vital organs are considered taken from deceased patients.

About a decade later, *Re A (A Minor)*[11] provided the courts with another opportunity to confirm DNC's legal status. This case involved a 19-month old infant, known as Child A, who was taken to hospital in December 1991 with bruising and fractures. He was treated at the hospital until the beginning of January 1992 but was brought back to hospital on 17 January 1992 as an emergency case. No heartbeat was detected. The next day, he was transferred to Guy's Hospital for intensive care and assessment. Child A was put on a ventilator and a brain scan showed blood, the distribution of which suggested that the child has had a non-accidental injury. On that same day, an emergency protection order was made under the Children Act 1989 giving parental responsibility of the child to the Local Authority.

On 21 January 1992, a Consultant paediatric neurologist concluded that A was brain stem dead.[12] The same tests were also carried out the next day by another Consultant paediatric neurologist who reached the same conclusion that A was brain stem dead. On 22 January 1992, the parents applied to a Family Proceedings Court for an order that "[n]o person with parental responsibility, namely the parents and the Local Authority, shall give consent to the switching off of a life support machine in respect of A without the consent of those others with parental responsibility after consultation with the *guardian ad litem*."[13] This was on the same day as when the medical team concluded that A was brain stem dead. The parents wanted A to continue to be ventilated so as to enable further medical tests to be conducted by medical experts instructed by the parents. The quality of the evidence, including as to the cause of the child's injuries and admission to hospital would be compromised if the ventilator was removed. The court was, however, of the opinion that the cause of injury was better served by *post mortem*.

---

[10] At pp. 179–180.

[11] [1992] 3 Med L.R. 303.

[12] Note the usage of the newer term here. Interestingly, it was used 3 years before the 1995 Review carried out by the Working Group of the Royal College of Physicians recommended that "brain stem death" is a more accurate description than "brain death". This seemed influenced by the term's deployment in the British Paediatric Association (BPA)'s Report in 1991—ibid., at p. 304.

[13] At p. 303.

Importantly, it observed that the precise definition of death was upon the recommendation of the professional bodies including the British Paediatric Association.[14] The court was satisfied that the Consultants had applied all the necessary criteria and each one was satisfied to come to a decision that Child A was brain stem dead. The judge stated that "I have no hesitation at all in holding that A has been dead since Tuesday of last week, January 21."[15] This signified that whilst medicine takes the time of death as the conclusion of the second test,[16] the legal time of death is when the first test confirmed brain stem death. He added that "I hold too that it would be wholly contrary to the interests of that child, as they may now be, for his body to be subjected to what would seem to me to be continuing indignity to which it is subject".[17] Thus although it was accepted that the child has died, he was said to still have interests in not having his body subjected to indignity. It was declared that should the hospital consider it appropriate to disconnect the child from the ventilator, they would not be acting contrary to the law. However, he did not consider it appropriate to make an order instructing the doctors to disconnect the ventilator. Significantly, it was clarified that it is not the function of the court to usurp the discretion of the medical team as to what they deemed appropriate in the circumstances. It is interesting to note that although organ donation was not an issue in the case, one of the Consultants said that had she been asked to advise whether it was proper for the child's organs to be removed, she would unhesitatingly clarify that A was brain stem dead.[18] Organ donation was therefore raised as a hypothetical point, but this had seemed more for the purpose of emphasising that Child A was clinically dead.

In 1993, the House of Lords (the predecessor of the Supreme Court), also seemed to express approval of DNC in the high profile case of *Airedale NHS Trust v. Bland*.[19] It is important to observe that the judges' comments took place in the context of a patient whose brain stem was still alive. The patient, Anthony Bland, was seriously injured in the Hillsborough Disaster and was diagnosed as being in a persistent vegetative state (PVS). When the case went to court, he had been in this condition for over 3 years and the medical team was of the view that there was no hope of any improvement in his condition or recovery. He was able to breathe on his own and had not therefore needed to be ventilated. He nevertheless needed round the clock care and was dependent on artificial nutrition and hydration. With the concurrence of his family, the hospital where he was treated sought declarations from the court that they might (a) lawfully discontinue all life-sustaining treatment and medical support measures designed to keep him alive; and (b) lawfully discontinue and thereafter withhold medical treatment except for the sole purpose of enabling him to die with

[14] As highlighted in Chap. 2, the BPA issued a Report in 1991 recommending that the criteria used to determine death for children over 2 months old who were comatose, totally apnoeic and being ventilated, should be the same as those used for adults.

[15] At p. 305.

[16] See the discussion in Chap. 2.

[17] At p. 305.

[18] At p. 304.

[19] [1993] AC 789.

the greatest dignity and the least of pain, suffering and distress. The House of Lords granted the declarations, but did so on the grounds other than that Bland was already dead.

In the course of the judgment, Lord Keith noted that "in the eyes of the medical world and of the law a person is not clinically dead so long as the brain stem retains its function".[20] Lord Goff stated that "as a result of developments in modern medical technology, doctors no longer associate death exclusively with breathing and heartbeat, and it has come to be accepted that death occurs when the brain, and in particular the brain stem, has been destroyed".[21] Similarly, Lord Browne-Wilkinson observed that "[i]n medicine, the cessation of breathing or of heartbeat is no longer death. By the use of a ventilator, lungs which in the unaided course of nature would have stopped breathing can be made to breathe, thereby sustaining the heartbeat... This has led the medical profession to redefine death in terms of brain stem death, i.e., the death of that part of the brain without which the body cannot function at all without assistance. In some cases it is now apparently possible, with the use of the ventilator, to sustain a beating heart even though the brain stem, and therefore in medical terms the patient is dead...".[22] However, as these comments were made "to illustrate the scale of the problem which is presented by modern technological developments,"[23] they were strictly *obiter*.[24]

3.2.2 The Calm Before the Storm

Subsequent cases proceeded on the basis that brain stem death is already an accepted and settled term for medical and legal purposes. An example can be seen in 1995 in *Cleveland County Council v. F and Others*,[25] a case relating to care proceedings of the surviving siblings of a 1-month old girl who died from non-accidental injury. When referring to the girl's death, the court simply mentioned that "[b]rain stem death was diagnosed and [the girl's] life support systems were turned off".[26] No further commentaries were provided on the definition of death. It is implicit from this that brain stem death is unquestionably the determinant of death upon which ventilator can be legally switched off. This can similarly be seen in 2000 in *R v. Her Majesty's Coroner for Coventry*,[27] concerning death in custody. The court stated that the deceased was "pronounced dead at 0930 on 6th August, although it is possible (but irrelevant) that brain stem death may have occurred somewhat earlier. In broad

[20] At p. 856.

[21] At p. 863.

[22] At p. 878.

[23] *Per* Lord Browne-Wilkinson at p. 878.

[24] Butler-Cole and Tankel (2020), paragraph 28.

[25] [1995] 1 WLR 785.

[26] At p. 787.

[27] 2000 WL 989, 473.

and lay terms, the cause of death was massive bleeding into the brain, causing both the formation of blood clots and enlargement of the brain itself. The resultant pressure caused downward displacement of the brain and in turn brain stem death."[28]

Then in 2002 in *R (John Smeaton on Behalf of Society for the Protection of Unborn Children) v. The Secretary of State for Health v Schering Health Care Ltd., Family Planning Association*,[29] a case which concerned the legality of the prescription, supply and use of the morning-after pill, the High Court stated plainly that "[o]nce upon a time the law, following medical science, treated death as marked by the cessation of breathing or of heartbeat. At present the law treats death as meaning brain stem death".[30] In 2003, in *R v. Morrison (Ian Stuart)*,[31] a case concerning an appeal over the length of a sentence for an unlawful killing, the Court of Appeal described the pronouncement of death as follows: "By the morning of 9th April [the victim] had suffered brain stem death. It was concluded that traumatic brain injury with cerebral oedema had led to irredeemable brain injury. He was pronounced dead later that morning".[32] Thus the court simply referred to the fact that the victim died after/when confirmed as brain stem dead at the hospital. It did not see it necessary to provide any commentaries on this.

In 2014, in *C (By His Father and Litigation Friend 'F') v. North Cumbria University Hospitals NHS Trust*,[33] a husband who testified about his wife's labour in a negligence claim against a midwife for his child's injury, said that "I was met by the anaesthetist who bid me, in a matter of fact way, that the brain stem death tests had been carried out that there were no sign of life and that no medication would help. He asked me, quite brusquely, when I wanted the life-support machine turned off."[34] The court did not examine whether the anaesthetist's question was appropriate, signifying that it did not see it problematic that termination of life-support intervention should follow confirmation of brain stem death. In the same year, the High Court of Ireland heard in the case of *P.P. v Health Service Executive*[35] a situation regarding a woman who had suffered brain stem death while pregnant. Her medical team decided to, *inter alia*, continue her ventilatory support; maintain her on heavy doses of medication for a number of conditions; and provide twice daily physiotherapy for the duration of her pregnancy. They also performed a tracheostomy to facilitate the continuation of maternal organ supportive measures in an effort to attain foetal viability. The pregnant woman's father found these measures unreasonable and brought the matter to court to have them discontinued. The court's approval of the medical profession's definition of death is discernible from this sentence: "[t]his unfortunate unborn has suffered the

---

28 At p. 1.

29 [2002] EWHC 610 (Admin).

30 *Per* Mr. Justice Munby at paragraph 57.

31 [2003] EWCA Crim 1953.

32 At paragraph 5.

33 [2014] EWHC 61 (QB).

34 At paragraph 17.

35 [2014] IEHC 622.

dreadful fate of being present in the womb of a mother who *has died*...".[36] Although Article 40.3 of the Irish Constitution acknowledges the right of the unborn and guarantees to defend and vindicate that right, the foetus in this case was only 15 weeks in gestation and was assessed as having a weak prospect of surviving. To maintain and continue the somatic support for the pregnant woman in those circumstances would, according to the court, deprive her of dignity in death. It therefore authorised, at the discretion of the medical team, the withdrawal of those support.

The cases above illustrate that courts have continued to endorse brain stem death as a legal definition of death. They have also stressed that while a brain stem dead person is deceased, they still retain an interest in having their bodies treated with dignity. A crucial aspect of this is not to have their bodies be subjected to continuous life-sustaining interventions. These should and could therefore be removed. Since case law did not deal directly with organ donation, would the continuation of such interventions be justified and legally condoned in the short period of time between confirmation of brain stem death and removal of vital organs from patients who are eligible to be organ donors? It would be interesting and useful to hear the judiciary's viewpoint on this, since heart-beating organ donation not only requires the maintenance of the said technology but also the performance of invasive procedures to remove organs from a body whose dignity they said needs to be protected. This is especially so since the procedures are carried out for the benefit of others rather than the donors.

3.2.3 Death: A Matter of Perspective?

If DNC went largely uncontested in the courtroom since mid-1990s, the last few years began to witness the emergence of cases which are not dissimilar to Jahi McMath's in the USA. One of these is *Re A (A Child)*[37] which was brought by the Central Manchester NHS Foundation Trust to the High Court. This case concerned a 19-month old child who, on 6 February 2015, choked on a tiny piece of fruit and became unconscious. He was rushed to the hospital and was in severe respiratory distress when he arrived. He was operated on immediately to remove the fruit and was transferred to paediatric intensive care where he remained fully ventilated. An MRI scan carried out the next day revealed that Child A had suffered extensive brain injury. On 10 February 2015, 2 brain stem tests were carried out—one in the morning (at 10.10 am), the other in the evening (at 5.30 pm). The results indicated that Child A was brain stem dead. The hospital therefore wanted to switch off the ventilator but this was objected to by his parents. They are Saudi nationals who were in the UK as Child A's father was studying for a Ph.D. degree. They objected, on religious grounds, to the plan to switch off the ventilator. As Muslims, they do not accept that brain stem death is synonymous with death from a religious viewpoint. In view of

[36] *Per* Kearns P. (emphasis added).

[37] [2015] EWHC 443.

the conflict, the hospital sought a declaration from the court that it would be lawful to discontinue and withdraw life-support interventions, including artificial ventilation, from Child A.

Mr. Justice Hayden, in his deliberations, took into consideration the Academy of the Medical Royal Colleges' *Code of Practice for the Diagnosis and Confirmation of Death*; and the conclusions and recommendations of the 1991 *Report of a Working Party of the British Paediatric Association on the Diagnosis of Brain-Stem Death in Infants and Children*. He expressed satisfaction that the confirmatory tests were conducted in accordance with well-established clinical guidelines. Concluding that the criteria for death was established by 10.10 am on 10 February 2015 (i.e. by reference to the first test), he granted the declaration sought by the hospital. In so doing, he rejected the parents' viewpoint that ventilation should be maintained as the child was still alive. He also rejected their alternative plea to be allowed to fly Child A back to Saudi Arabia with the ventilator maintained. The parents highlighted that life support treatment would never be switched off in Saudi Arabia for religious reasons and they wanted his care to continue in a Saudi medical facility.

Referring to the patient as "Child A's body",[38] Mr. Justice Hayden stressed that "the time has now come to permit the ventilator to be turned off and to allow Child A, who died on 10th February, dignity in death".[39] Expressing his sympathy for the family, he nevertheless made it clear that the child was already dead. Concerned that Child A's body should no longer be allowed to be subjected to the indignities that it was subjected to, he allowed the doctors to switch off the ventilator and remove all LST. He nevertheless refrained from making an order to this effect. This case was therefore decided in a manner which is consistent with earlier judgements as regards the legal acceptability of brain stem death. Space, however, did not seem to have been created for religious objection to DNC.[40]

This was replicated in the 2019 case of *Oxford University NHS Trust v. AB (A Minor), CD and EF*.[41] This case concerned a 14-year old girl, AB, who was found hanging at home on 17 October 2019. When she eventually received medical attention, her brain had already been deprived of oxygen for at least 31 min. She was placed on mechanical ventilation and was subsequently diagnosed as brain stem dead by 2 doctors, the first test completed at 10.26 am on 22 October 2019. The Oxford University Hospital Trust sought declaration from the High Court that (a) the criteria for death have been established; and (b) it is lawful and in AB's best interests for all care and treatment to be withdrawn. The court therefore needed to decide on whether she has died and when this took place; and whether care and treatment should be withdrawn. Her parents, who are devout Christians, objected to the termination, pointing out that one important tenet of their faith is that it is wrong to kill another human being.

---

[38] At paragraph 25.

[39] At paragraph 26.

[40] Choong and Rady (2018) at 85–86.

[41] [2019] EWHC 3516 (Fam).

Mr. Justice Francis declared that AB was already dead according to the definition and criteria outlined by the Code of Practice issued by the Academy of Medical Royal Colleges in 2008. The legal time of death was confirmed as 10.26 am on 22 October 2019. This was followed by a declaration that it was therefore "lawful and in AB's best interests"[42] for all care and treatment to be halted. Like *R v. Malcherek; R v. Steel*, the judge did not look at the withdrawal of LST as an act of killing. While he understood that one of the basic tenets of the parents' religion is that it is wrong for one person to kill another, he emphasised that the hospital's application is "not about killing: it is about removing a ventilator which is artificially sustaining a heart".[43] He ended his judgment by acknowledging that this was neither the first nor will it be the last case where faith has conflicted with science.[44] However, just as in the case of *Re A (A Child)*, the court did not engage fully with the religious perspective on death, particularly as to whether it coheres with DNC.

Shortly after the case was decided, the High Court was confronted with a similar case. *Manchester University NHS Foundation Trust v. Namiq, Ali & Namiq*[45] concerned an infant named Midrar Namiq. Born full-term on 18th September 2019, his mother's membrane ruptured enroute to hospital and there was a cord prolapse, which deprived oxygen to his brain. He had no detectable heart rate nor any respiratory output when he was born. After his heart was restarted, he was placed on mechanical ventilation in the neonatal ICU (NICU) of the Manchester University Hospital NHS Foundation Trust. 3 brain stem death tests have been carried out, with each concluding that Midrar was brain stem dead. The first two were carried out on the 1st and 2nd of October respectively by 2 doctors. The hospital wished to switch off the ventilator but his parents protested. They made reference to their religious belief as Muslims and insisted on the continuation of ventilatory support. On 26 November 2019, the hospital sought a declaration from the High Court that it would be lawful for them to withdraw the ventilator to allow Midrar a kind and dignified death. Midrar was joined as a party to the proceedings and a guardian was also appointed for him.

Mrs. Justice Lieven set her task as follows: "The issue I have to decide is whether Midrar is dead, according to DNC as set out in the clinical guidance, and therefore the ventilator can be removed."[46] "The test for whether a patient is dead", it was clarified, "is in the first instance one for medical professionals"[47] and "[t]he legal question is one of the application of the DNC criteria".[48] Given Midrar's age when the brain stem tests were conducted, it was highlighted that *The Diagnosis of Death by Neurological Criteria in Infants Less than 2 Months Old: Updated Recommendations* produced by the Royal College of Paediatrics and Child Health would need to be considered

[42] At paragraph 3.

[43] At paragraph 13.

[44] At paragraph 23.

[45] [2020] EWHC 5 (Fam).

[46] At paragraph 4.

[47] At paragraph 31.

[48] At paragraph 32.

alongside the Academy of Medical Royal Colleges' 2008 Code of Practice. Both of these documents, she expressed approvingly, "were drawn up after a thorough and careful process by a body of highly competent experts".[49] If confirmed brain stem dead, the patient is deemed to have irreversibly lost life. As 3 DNC tests were undertaken, and with each confirming that Midrar was brain stem dead, a declaration was made that it was lawful for the hospital to withdraw the infant's mechanical ventilation. The time and date of death were confirmed as the conclusion of the first test, namely 20:01 on 1 October 2019.

Although Midrar's father claimed that occasionally, some signs of life were noticed, Mrs. Justice Lieven opined that whilst "it is perfectly understandable that the parents should cling to hope by pointing to Midrar's movements, including chest movements",[50] these were spinal cord reflexes. She added that the father's "desire to cling on to any hope does appear to have led him to interpret material in the way he wanted rather than at times listening to the evidence".[51] Thus the reaction of the father, himself a biomedical scientist,[52] was dismissed as that of a distressed parent who had difficulty accepting reality. Their religious concerns around how death is clinically determined were, just as in the previous 2 cases, not addressed.

The parents, without delay, made an application for permission to appeal. The Court of Appeal began its deliberations, in a case that is now identified as *Re M (Declaration of Death of Child)*,[53] with a detailed examination of the relevant provisions of the 2008 Code of Practice and the 2015 Guidance. The Court stated that Mrs. Justice Lieven has correctly identified that the issue that needs to be determined is one which centred on whether Midrar Namiq was dead, according to the DNC tests outlined in those documents, and if so, whether the ventilator could be removed. Satisfied that Midrar was brain stem dead in accordance with the criteria outlined, the permission to appeal was refused. To the extent that this outcome is predictable, given the similar tendency on the part of the courts since the early 1980s, it is hardly noteworthy. What is most interesting about the judgment, however, are the following points.

The first is the Court of Appeal's response to the submission made by Lord Brennan QC who presented the parents' case. His submission, which is worth quoting in full, is as follows: "The appropriate judicial approach is to determine whether the medical practice relied upon is accepted by a responsible body of relevant medical opinion; and then whether it is reasoned and logical; and then whether it reasonably and reliably reflects an acceptable risk/benefit for the child namely in a death case where the loss of consciousness and breathing are irreversible, i.e. not reversible nor alterable in time to come, so that the decision to stop mechanical ventilation must be based on a secure, safe and firm based conclusion of irreversibility due to brain stem death such that there is no alternative but an order to stop mechanical

[49] At paragraph 34.

[50] At paragraph 60.

[51] At paragraph 38.

[52] BBC News (2020).

[53] [2020] EWCA Civ 164.

ventilation. That requires careful, detailed and objective assessment of the medical practice relied upon."[54] To this, he added that for that approach to be both responsible and reasonable, the medical practice in other countries needs to be considered. He drew the court's attention to a number of jurisdictions that based their diagnosis of death on the wider concept of whole brain death, and how they require more tests to be carried out before death is determined.[55]

The Court of Appeal was thus invited to examine the robustness of the diagnosis and criteria currently used in the UK. However, the court responded in the following terms: "[a]s a matter of law, it is the case that brain stem death is established as the legal criteria in the United Kingdom by the House of Lords' decision in *Bland*. It is not, therefore, open to this court to contemplate a different test."[56] It continued: "it is, in reality, impossible for this court now to embark upon an assessment of whether a different test, namely that adopted in the USA, should replace the long established UK criteria represented in modern times by the 2008 Code and the 2015 Guidance".[57] In so finding, the court seemed to have elevated the *obiter* statement in *Bland* to a binding precedent. It also did not think that it is its place to assess whether the approaches adopted elsewhere is preferable to the one used in the UK.

Secondly, the court clarified that once a patient is confirmed brain stem dead, hence clinically and legally dead, the concept of "best interests" ceases to have any legal relevance.[58] This concept is only pertinent when considering the medical treatment of those who are still alive, be they children or adults who lack capacity.[59] In view of this, the court considered that Mr. Justice Francis inadvertently fell into error when he made reference to AB's best interests in *Oxford University NHS Trust v. AB (A Minor), CD and EF*. It is nonetheless important to note that while best interests is no longer a consideration once a diagnosis of brain stem death is confirmed, the patient still has an interest in being treated with dignity.

Thirdly, the court commended the approach taken by Mr. Justice Hayden in *Re A (A Minor)* as "the correct structure for dealing with sensitive applications of this nature".[60] The form of words employed in the case should thenceforth be used when courts are faced with situations such as the present. A declaration should therefore: expressly declare that the patient has died at a particular time and date; then give permission and declare that it is lawful for mechanical ventilation and other clinical interventions to be withdrawn; and identify that the purpose of the declaration was to allow the patient who had died "dignity in death".[61]

[54] At paragraph 63.

[55] At paragraph 64.

[56] At paragraph 91.

[57] At paragraph 92.

[58] At paragraph 49; Choong (2022) at 109.

[59] At paragraph 24.

[60] At paragraph 42.

[61] At paragraph 60.

It was soon applied in the 2022 case of *Barts Health NHS Trust v. Dance, Battersbee and Battersbee*.[62] The facts are rather unique in that the Academy's brain stem tests were not able to be performed. The background to the case is as follows. A 12-year old child by the name of Archie Battersbee was found suspended by his neck from his family home bannister on 7 April 2022. An ambulance was called but by the time he arrived at Southend Hospital, he has had a cardiac arrest and his brain has been starved of oxygen and blood supply for several minutes. An MRI scan was carried out and he was transferred to the Royal London Hospital the next day. Whilst there, doctors wanted to carry out brain stem tests but his family refused to provide consent. A court order to perform the tests were sought by the hospital and this was granted. However, doctors found that it was not possible to carry out the tests as Archie did not react to the peripheral nerve stimulation tests which were a precursor to the brain stem tests. Any outcome would therefore only provide a false negative result. Instead they proceeded to conduct another MRI scan on 31 May 2022. By then, Archie has already been subjected to numerous other tests including EEG and a CT angiogram. The MRI scan showed severe brain injury including over 50% damage to the brain stem. The hospital wanted to withdraw his mechanical ventilation. This was opposed by the parents who argued, *inter alia*, that they would like him to die naturally in the hospital as that is in line with their and Archie's Christian faith. To them, death occurs when the heart stops beating. In view of this, the hospital sought a declaration from the High Court that Archie is brain stem dead and that he was dead on a particular date; and that if the court is not able to make that finding, then the court should consider whether it is lawful and in Archie's best interests for his ventilation to be continued.

According to Mrs. Justice Arbuthnot, the decision in *Re M (Declaration of Death of Child)* made clear that the test for death is settled"[63] and that "[she] must apply the brain stem tests as [she is] bound by the House of Lords decision in *Bland*. There is no authority which has followed *Bland* which suggests [she] should adopt a different test".[64] Although the court did not have results from brain stem tests prescribed by the Academy, the judge held that "very severe brain damage does not prevent me from anxiously considering the abundant clinical evidence" and come to the conclusion that Archie was brain stem dead on the balance of probabilities. She made the following declaration, using the structure propounded in *Re M (Declaration of Death of Child)*, but without mentioning dignity in death: "I find that Archie dies on noon at 31st May 2022, which was shortly after the MRI scans taken that day. I find that irreversible cessation of brain stem function has been conclusively established.[65] I give permission to the medical professionals at the Royal London Hospital (1) to cease to ventilate mechanically Archie Battersbee; (2) to extubate Archie Battersbee; (3) to cease the administration of medication to Archie Battersbee and (4) not to

62 [2022] EWHC 1435 (Fam).

63 At paragraphs 152 and 153.

64 At paragraph 154.

65 At paragraph 180.

attempt any cardio or pulmonary resuscitation on Archie Battersbee when cardiac output ceases or respiratory effort ceased."[66]

As with the previous three cases, the court did not engage in any meaningful sense with the religious arguments. Similarly, neither was organ transplantation part of the issues in contention, other than the fact that the question of donation seemed to have been broached by a Consultant within days of Archie's arrival at the hospital which the family found upsetting.[67]

Unlike those previous cases, pronouncement of death was made without the benefit of the Academy's brain stem tests having been conducted. This was soon rectified by the Court of Appeal[68] to bring the case in line with the approach in *Re M (Declaration of Death of Child)* and earlier cases. According to the Court, the High Court judge had erred in making a declaration of death without the brain stem tests prescribed by the Academy's Code of Practice having been conducted. Mrs. Justice Arbuthnot should have instead proceeded to a best interests assessment once it was apparent that a brain stem test could not be performed. The presiding judges namely Sir Geoffrey Vos, Sir Andrew McFarlane and Lady Justice King[69] cautioned "judges in future cases of this kind from being drawn into attempting to declare death on a basis outside the Code where none of the medical witnesses has themselves made a diagnosis of death".[70]

The case was remitted to the High Court, where Mr. Justice Hayden was asked to determine Archie's best interests. He began his judgement by re-emphasising that "[a]scertaining death requires the application of clear clinical guidelines. Where they are not met, brain stem death cannot be identified with the certainty that such a conclusion requires".[71] The case therefore proceeded in this Court on the basis that Archie was still alive. Having set out the medical evidence which confirmed that his prognosis is extremely poor, the court assessed Archie's best interests by considering his personality, wishes, religious belief and needs, and the views of those caring for him. Mr. Justice Hayden reached the conclusion that continuation of ventilation was not in Archie's best interests, and the court held that it cannot authorise or declare lawful its continuation.[72]

Permission to appeal was immediately applied for by the parents. The grounds for appeal centred around whether the High Court had taken into proper account Archie's best interests in the widest sense rather than "driven almost wholly"[73] by the child's medical best interests. The judges unanimously dismissed permission to appeal. According to the Court of Appeal, "[w]hilst it is, most sadly, correct that it

---

[66] At paragraph 181.

[67] At paragraph 100.

[68] *Barts Health NHS Trust v. Dance, Battersbee and Battersbee* [2022] EWCA Civ 935.

[69] Note that two of the judges (namely Sir Andrew McFarlane and Lady Justice King) also presided over the case of *Re M (Declaration of Death of Child)*.

[70] At paragraph 37.

[71] *Barts Health NHS Trust v. Dance, Battersbee and Battersbee* [2022] EWFC 80 at paragraph 2.

[72] At paragraph 46.

[73] *Dance and Battersbee v. Barts Health NHS Trust and Battersbee* [2022] EWCA Civ 1055 at paragraph 23.

was the medical evidence that ultimately determined the outcome of the judge's best interests determination, [Mr. Justice Hayden] had clearly taken full account of the countervailing factors. Those factors, and in particular Archie's individual feelings and religious beliefs, were insufficient to avoid a finding that the continuation of life-sustaining treatment was no longer in the best interests of this moribund child ...]".[74] Importantly for present purposes, the fact that the arguments centred around best interests indicate that the Court of Appeal continued to proceed on the basis that Archie was still alive. When the parents filed an application to appeal to the Supreme Court, this was refused by the Supreme Court as "the application does not raise an arguable point of law that the Court of Appeal has fallen into error in exercising its discretion in the way in which it did".[75]

The *Battersbee* case confirmed that the brain stem death tests prescribed by the 2008 Code of Practice (and where relevant the 2015 Guidance) must be performed before death is confirmed. If the tests have not been conducted, the patient cannot be pronounced dead. Instead, a best interests assessment should be undertaken in which the patient's welfare would be considered in its widest sense.

3.3 Conclusion

Although there is no statutory definition of death in the UK, it has been lawful to determine death using neurological criteria almost from the start of its medical journey. This is attributable to the continuous recognition and support given by the judiciary to the professional bodies' definition and criteria throughout the last few decades.

Several trends and tendencies are discernible in the approach taken. For one, the judiciary do not seem to have demonstrated any reservation, much less palpable resistance, to the new medical definition of death. This accepting and unquestioning attitude can be detected from the beginning. In the 1981 joint cases of *R v Malcherek*; *R v Steel*, which were decided not long after brain death made the transition from being an indicator of futility to that of clinical death, the judiciary did not query why the criteria previously used to pronounce medical futility were soon after used to pronounce death. Rather, the judgement referred to the criteria used as those which were "generally accepted"[76] by the medical profession. It is worth remembering that this characterisation came a mere 2 years after the Academy of Medical Royal Colleges released their 1979 Addendum. This holds implications for heart-beating donation, which was made legal by extension, since organs are taken from patients deemed dead.

[74] At paragraph 71.

[75] Supreme Court (2022). At the time the manuscript was submitted for publication, it was reported that Archie's parents have requested the UN Committee on the Rights of Persons With Disabilities (UNRPD) to consider the case—see Anonymous (2022) .

[76] At 181.

Further, when dispute arose as to whether the patient was dead and whether ventilation can thereby be removed or has been legally removed, the judiciary framed their task as one to determine if the patient has died according to the definition and criteria set out by the medical profession. If so, ventilation can be removed or has been legally removed. Hence rather than asking how death should be defined or whether the UK's version of DNC is sufficiently robust for purposes of determining death, the courts' starting point is to ask how doctors determine death. If the definition and criteria used by doctors confirmed that clinical death has occurred, then legal death has also occurred. By viewing their task in this manner, the medical profession's definition and criteria for determining death are therefore embraced wholesale and not subjected to critical scrutiny. Provided a diagnosis of death was made by reference to the documents issued by the professional bodies, judges have been satisfied that death has occurred. As stated by the Court of Appeal in *R v. Malcherek*; *R v. Steel*, "[i]t is no part of the task of this court to inquire whether the criteria, the Royal Medical College confirmatory tests, are a satisfactory code of practice".[77] Forty years later, a similar sentiment was expressed by the Court of Appeal in *Re M (Declaration of Death)*. To reiterate Sir Andrew McFarlane, "it is impossible for this court now to embark upon an assessment of whether a different test…should replace the long established UK criteria represented in modern times by the 2008 Code and the 2015 Guidance".[78] As highlighted, judges are even willing to accept confirmation of tests conducted according to those guidelines on occasions when not all the specified tests were carried out as long as reasons were tendered as to why certain tests were not conducted.

To a large extent, the propensities above are understandable given the highly technical nature of defining death neurologically.[79] However, they also illustrate that the judiciary were content to leave the matter of how death is defined to the medical profession. This has inadvertently (or perhaps advertently) resulted in other approaches to death to be sidelined in the courtroom. In particular, space was not adequately created for arguments made on religious grounds. It is noteworthy that none of the recent cases where religious objections were raised made any mention of the Jahi McMath case, nor of similar cases from other jurisdictions where religion has been afforded a more sympathetic hearing. Further, the courts were also reluctant to consider the DNC frameworks used in other jurisdictions.

The judiciary nevertheless differ from the medical profession as regards the time of death. In relation to the 2 tests which the professional bodies have specified for diagnosing brain stem death, courts have proclaimed the conclusion of the first test as the legal time of death. The second test is, from a legal viewpoint, merely confirmatory. Upon a diagnosis of brain stem death, the courts accept that death has occurred, and being dead, those patients no longer have any best interests that need to be protected. The courts held that they nevertheless still have an interest in not having their bodies subjected to indignity. One source of indignity is the continuation of

[77] At 179.

[78] At paragraph 92.

[79] Munoz and Fox (2013) at 22.

artificial ventilation of what the courts have, by that stage, considered as a dead body or a corpse. Where declarations have been sought that the withdrawal and cessation of artificial ventilation and life-sustaining treatment were lawful, courts have therefore been willing to grant them. By the same token, they do not consider the removal of artificial ventilation as something which kills the patient, as the ventilator is merely sustaining a lifeless patient's lungs and heart. It is nevertheless interesting to note that courts have not gone beyond this remit of granting declarations to actually make an order that the ventilation and life-sustaining treatment be withdrawn. They have remained respectful to, and are not willing to usurp, the medical teams' discretion.

It is clear that the cases which have thus far come before the courts are not factually and directly concerned with organ donation. Thus unlike the emergence of the medical definition of death, the legal endorsement of DNC does not seem entangled with nor influenced by a desire to advance organ transplantation. It was prompted instead by concerns over the legal status of brain stem dead patients before ventilators are switched off. That notwithstanding, this legal development has strong implications for the field. Since brain stem dead patients are legally dead, removal of vital organs from their bodies would not be an act that kills them. Heart-beating organ donation would therefore not contravene the dead donor rule. However, if the courts held that there is dignity in death, and continuation of ventilation on a deceased person is an undignified imposition, would the preservation of heartbeat and circulation via ventilation until organs are harvested not denying the deceased patient dignity in death? Further, would the invasive procedures involved in organ removal not be an additional and even graver denial of this? After all, are they not "operations which 'mutilate' the donor for the advantage of another person?"[80] It is clear from this, that while judicial pronouncements made for one purpose would have implications for other areas, some of the reasonings would not be an appropriate fit for the latter.

The next chapter will explore the limitations of courtroom deliberations and the comparative advantage of Parliamentary law-making in negotiating DNC's legal status.

References

Anonymous. 1963. Man Kept Alive as Kidney Donor: Death After the Brawl. *The Times* 26 July

Anonymous. 2022. UN Request for Archie Battersbee Life-Support to Continue. *BBC News*, 29 July.

BBC News. 2020. Midrar Ali: Dad of Baby Boy in Legal Battle "Pressured" by Medics. Available at https://www.bbc.co.uk/news/uk-england-manchester-51209077.

Butler-Cole, V., and B. Tankel. 2020. Brain Death and the Law (February). Available at https://www.mentalcapacitylawandpolicy.org.uk/wp-content/uploads/2020/03/Brain-death-talk-VBQC.pdf.

[80] Wolstenholme and O'Connor (1966), p. viii, cited in M. Lock, 'Inventing a New Death and Making it Believable' (2002) 9(2) *Anthropology and Medicine* 97–115 at 102.

Choong, K.A., and M.Y. Rady. 2018. Re A (A Child) and the United Kingdom Code of Practice for the Diagnosis and Confirmation of Death: Should a Secular Construct of Death Override Religious Values in a Pluralistic Society? *HEC Forum* 71–89.

Choong, K.A. 2022. Re M (Declaration of Death of Child) [2010]: "No Best Interests to Consider"? In *Culture and Law: Multidisciplinary Cross-Fertilization of Views on the End of Life*, ed. S. Rohlfing-Dijoux, and U. Hellmann, 105–114. Baden-Baden: Nomos. https://doi.org/10.5771/9783748921271-105.

Munoz, R.T., and M.D. Fox. 2013. Legal Aspects of Brain Death and Organ Donorship. In *The Brain-Dead Organ Donor: Pathophysiology and Management*, ed. D. Novitzky, and D.K.C. Cooper, 21–36. New York: Springer.

Supreme Court. 2022. Permission to Appeal Decision in the Matter of Archie Battersbee, 28 July 2022. Available at https://www.supremecourt.uk/news/permission-to-appeal-decision-in-the-matter-of-archie-battersbee.html.

Wolstenholme G.E.W., and M. O'Connor. 1966. Ethics in Medical Progress: With Special Reference to Transplantation. Boston: Little, Brown and Co., cited in Lock, M. 2002. Inventing a New Death and Making it Believable. *Anthropology and Medicine* 9 (2): 97–115 at 102.

Chapter 4
Democratising Death

Abstract Although diagnosis of death by neurological criteria (DNC) has received judicial endorsement since the 1980s, courts have sidelined requests made in recent cases to consider a broader range of methods to determine death. Those pleas were made on the grounds that the definition and criteria espoused by the medical profession in the UK are dissimilar to those used in other jurisdictions that also adopt DNC; and that faith communities have a different understanding of death. This chapter takes a close look at those other approaches before highlighting the inherent limitations of the courtroom as the forum for forging the legitimacy of DNC. It puts forward the argument that the democratic process should instead be engaged, by reviewing the comparative advantage of Parliamentary law-making

Keywords Whole brain death · Brain stem death · Diversity · Democracy · Abrahamic faith · Courtroom · Parliament

4.1 Introduction

Determination of death using neurological criteria has received judicial endorsement in a succession of cases since the 1980s. In the process, the courts have sidelined requests put forward in a number of recent cases to consider a broader range of methods to determine death. Those pleas were made on the grounds that the definition and criteria espoused by the medical profession in the UK are dissimilar to those used in other jurisdictions that also adopt DNC; and that faith communities have a different understanding of death. This chapter takes a closer look at those other approaches before highlighting the inherent limitations of the courtroom as the forum for forging the legitimacy of the new method of diagnosing death. It then assesses the comparative advantage of Parliamentary law-making particularly in relation to the two issues given insufficient consideration by the courts. In so doing, it puts forward the view that for a matter as significant as how death is determined in ICUs and neurological centres, the democratic process should be engaged.

K. A. Choong, *The Medico-Legal Development of Neurological Death in the UK*,
https://doi.org/10.1007/978-981-19-6763-4_4

4.2 Diversity in Death

DNC has, as examined in the previous chapter, enjoyed uncritical acceptance by the courts. Meanwhile, pleas to consider other approaches to death have largely been dismissed. This part of the discussion will firstly illustrate how the definition, criteria and protocol used by the medical profession in the UK are not necessarily shared by other jurisdictions which also accept neurological death. It then looks at how faith communities understand death.

4.2.1 DNC: Lack of International Consensus

Many countries around the world have now accepted and adopted brain-based determination of death. The 2 formulations of DNC which have been widely used are whole brain death and brain stem death.[1] The former is a conceptual definition which equates the complete and permanent damage to the whole brain (which includes the brain stem) with the death of the person. The latter is a conceptual definition which asserts that destruction of the brain stem alone is equivalent to the death of a person.[2] Common to both are the fundamental assumptions that the body has a localised critical system, and this critical system is the brain.[3]

Studies have shown that there is considerable variability in the criteria and practice employed even among jurisdictions that adopt the same formulation.[4] For instance, many but not all, indicated that it is necessary to identify a cause for catastrophic brain injury before a DNC determination is carried out.[5] There is also a lack of consistency in the components identified for the clinical examination of DNC. Many, but not all, include coma, pupillary reflex, corneal reflex, oculovestibular reflex, gag reflex, cough reflex, and oculocephalic reflex. Meanwhile, a small number include noxious stimulation to the face, noxious stimulation to the limbs and other reflexes. Even so, the description of the technique, findings and conditions which could affect the outcomes of those assessments differ across jurisdictions.[6] Further, some type of ancillary testing is required in some, but not all, countries.[7] Also at variance is the number of examiners required for diagnosing death. Some require only 1 examiner,

[1] Greer et al. (2020) at 1081.

[2] Spears et al. (2022). Unlike the former, a brain stem dead patient may still have some cortical electrical activity or intracranial blood flow—see Smith (2012) at i7.

[3] Shewmon (1998) at 126 .

[4] E.g. Lewis et al. (2020); Robbins and Bernat (2018); D.M. Greer, et al., op. cit., Sprung et al. (2014); Shemie et al. (2014); Chua et al. (2015); Cameron et al. (2016).

[5] A. Lewis, et al., ibid., p. e301.

[6] Ibid., p. e302.

[7] D. M. Greer et al., op. cit., p. 1081; N. M. Robbins and J. L. Bernat, op. cit., pp. 266–272.

while others require 2 or more.[8] This inconsistency extends to the mandatory credential of the examiner or at least one of the examiners. These range from a neurologist, a neurosurgeon, a licensed doctor, an anaesthesiologist, an intensivist, and the doctor in charge of the hospital.[9] The length of time the examiner(s) need to have been in practice also differs.[10] The same goes for the number of examinations required to declare DNC. Some indicated a need for 2 or more examinations to be performed, while others did not address this point. Of those requiring 2 or more examinations, a majority expect these to be conducted consecutively separated by a range of 1–72 h.[11]

The time of death too was not specified in the protocols of some jurisdictions. Of those that were, time of death is either on completion of clinical examination, the time an ancillary test was interpreted, the time an ancillary test was performed, or at another time.[12] Further, some countries' protocols do not specify age groups; while some address only adults with no specified age. Others address newborns and older; or those who are over: 1 month old; 1 year old; 2 years; or another age before 18.[13] Of these, some have 2 age brackets while some have 3–5 or more age brackets, with the criteria for determining DNC varying across brackets. These may involve the time between examinations, the observation period, the number of examiners and examinations, blood pressure prerequisite, temperature prerequisite, ancillary testing indications, apnoea testing technique, and others. In addition, while many countries' protocols specify that those performing a determination of DNC should not be a member of the transplantation teams, others do not make this explicit.[14]

This lack of consensus is attributable to the fact that the process of redefining death was not coordinated as part of an international endeavour. Rather, they developed gradually on an *ad hoc* basis in one interested country after another.[15] The presence of more than one formulation of death, and the deployment of a multitude of practices and processes to determine DNC highlight that the UK's approach to DNC is but one among many. That this is the case underlines the significance of a public debate as to the robustness of the definition and criteria currently used. Before this issue is explored, another neglected element of diversity will be examined.

4.2.2 Religious Perspective

Looking next at how death is understood from a religious perspective, the focus would be on the Abrahamic faith traditions from whose communities the majority of

[8] A. Lewis et al., op. cit., p. e301.

[9] Ibid.

[10] D. M. Greer, op. cit., p. 1090.

[11] A. Lewis et al., op. cit., p. e301.

[12] Ibid., pp. e304–e305.

[13] Ibid., p. e301.

[14] Ibid.

[15] Lock (1996) at 577.

the cases in the UK and North America arose. The discussion below will therefore consider the positions in Judaism, Christianity and Islam.[16] When discussing the issue of death within these religious communities, it is necessary to note that there is a lack of consensus among various denominations, religious leaders and scholars regarding the acceptability of DNC.[17] While there are those within these faith traditions who accept DNC, the discussion below will draw attention to those with an opposing viewpoint, as these are the main sources of legal contention. The discussion will consider their positions as regards withdrawal of ventilation and removal of vital organs.

Adherents of the Abrahamic faith traditions believe in the existence of the soul. This concept has been described as the spiritual essence of a person which continues in a disembodied state after death.[18] It is an entity which endows the human with an intellect, emotions, a will, and an autonomous sense of self.[19] Although it is understood that death occurs when the soul vacates the body, there is a lack of clarity over when this metaphysical phenomenon happens as it cannot be observed directly.[20] Desoulment cannot, therefore, readily provide a basis of a legal or medical test.[21] Equally, since there does not seem to be any indications in religious scriptures that the soul resides exclusively in the brain, whole brain death or brain stem death cannot therefore convincingly lead to the conclusion that the body and soul have separated.[22] Rather, it has been pointed out that the soul still inhabits the body as long as breath is still present or while the body is still alive.

In Judaism, for instance, reference is often made to the following passage from the Talmud, when establishing the time of death: "If a house collapses and buries a man within, we are required to remove the debris in an attempt to find him, even if it is the Sabbath.[23] When he is found, he is examined up to his nose."[24] Only when no sign of life, namely respiration, was detected would the person's death be halachically established and rescue work be discontinued.[25] Thus even if the respiration is extremely shallow, the person is still considered alive and work must continue to extricate the man completely, since "all in whose nostrils was the breath of the spirit of life".[26] In Christianity, the interconnection between the breath and

[16] For discussions of the viewpoints of other religions, see e.g., Setta and Shemie (2015) ; Alhawari et al. (2020)., Organ Transplantation .

[17] See e.g., Padela et al. (2013); Napier (2009); Breshnahan and Mahler (2010); Ashkenazi et al. (2015); Haas (2011); Miller (2016).

[18] Herring (2021), p. 180; Moreland , p. 1.

[19] Disney and Poston (2010) at 273.

[20] Hussain (2022) at 19; Canadian Catholic Bioethics Institute, p. 6.

[21] J. Herring, op. cit., p. 180.

[22] Verheijde and Potts (2010) at 248 .

[23] Clearing debris was ordinarily considered work and thereby prohibited on the Sabbath—see Gabbay and Fins (2019) at 1676 .

[24] The Talmud: Yoma, 85a.

[25] Tendler (1996), pp. 32–33.

[26] Genesis 7:22 in Jütte (2021), p. 232.

the soul was made clear in the Bible: "And the Lord God formed man of the dust of the ground, and breathed into his nostrils the breath of life; and man became a living soul".[27] Since the living human being is an integrated unity of body and soul while the body is alive or continues to function in an integrated manner, there is no reason to assume that the body-soul unity has been dissolved.[28] This is so even if the person is not able to exercise the full range of human abilities.[29] Similarly in Islam, the Quran explained that the Almighty "made the human in proportion, and breathed into him the soul (created by the Almighty for that person)' .[30] To the extent that the nourishment of the soul is air, the absence or presence of respiration is the indicator of whether the soul has left the human body or otherwise.[31] Put another way, the soul maintains its relation to the body through the breath. Thus it is only when respiration ends that the soul is separated from the body.[32]

The discussion above shows that there is a strong association between breathing and the presence of life from a faith perspective. Hence whilst some of their co-religionists may have accepted neurological death, others claim that the soul may still inhabit the body as long as the person is still breathing. This would be the case even if the breathing and heartbeat were aided by medical intervention.[33] It is prohibited to hasten the death of a person in this state by withdrawing mechanical ventilation and life-support since any fraction of life, in whatever state of animation or whatever its quality, still has a value from a religious perspective.[34] Thus if ventilation is switched off upon a diagnosis of neurological death, it is this which arguably leads to the departure of the soul, hence the demise of the person. By extension, it is also forbidden to remove vital organs from heart-beating donors as this is considered a procurement of organs from people who are still alive.[35] Indeed such an act would be the proximate cause of the person's death.[36] This violates the sacredness of human life, even if the act was motivated by the desire to delay the death or save the life of other individuals.[37] Vital organs can only be excised when the donors are "in fact truly (not just "clinically") dead."[38] For those who find neurological death misaligned with their faith, the traditional method of cessation of breathing and heartbeat is

27 The Bible: Genesis, 2:7.

28 J. L. Verheijde and M. Potts, op. cit., p. 249.

29 Jones (2012) at 136 .

30 The Quran: As-Sajdah, 9.

31 Bedir and Aksoy (2011) at 291.

32 Ibid.

33 R. Jutte, op. cit., p. 233.

34 Jacobovits (1980) at 60; Shomali (2008).

35 Alhawari et al. (2020) at 1208 ; Verheijde et al. (2018) at 1756–1759.

36 E. Gabbay and J. J. Fins, op. cit., p. 1676; Rady and Verheijde (2013) at 33 ; Alexander (2019) at 325.

37 O'Rourke and Boyle (2011), p. 120; Nguyen (2017) at 159; The Quran: Surah Al-Maidah, 32.

38 I. Jacobovits, op. cit., p. 63.

accepted as a reliable method for determining life's endpoint, namely that the soul has departed.[39]

Having explored the divergences among jurisdictions which adopt DNC, and how religious communities view death, the work will now identify why courtrooms are not the most conducive venue for legitimising DNC in general, and for handling diversity in death, in particular.

4.3 Limitations of Judicial Decision-Making

Next to Acts of Parliament, judge-made case law is undoubtedly an important source of law. However, the ways in which these are produced are fundamentally different. The judiciary, established and empowered by the State as a legal institution to adjudicate legal disputes,[40] perform this role by responding to the factual situations brought before them. They listen to and deliberate on, the proofs and reasoned arguments presented by the disputing parties; and accommodate their procedures to the problems before them.[41] Their judgements are consequently tied to the facts to be decided.[42] The policy issues, larger public interests and wider repercussions at stake are not in contemplation when their decisions were made.[43] This is partly due to their being ill-equipped to undertake a wide-ranging analysis of the socio-economic consequences of their decisions,[44] and partly owing to resource and time constraints. Although expert witnesses can be called to court to testify, this too is restricted in a number of ways. They are only asked to address issues pertinent to the case at hand. As they are, in an adversarial system, often selected by the parties themselves on the basis that they would support their case, the views expressed can be one-sided or partisan.[45] The numbers that can be called too are limited on grounds of costs and time. In short, the adversarial system does not ensure that the court is presented with the best expert thinking on a subject.[46] Further, representatives of other people whose lives could be directly or indirectly affected by the decision, are not called upon to testify. Also absent from the courtroom is informed public debate and participation

---

39 A. Hussain, op. cit., p. 19; Editorial (2011) .

40 Neudorf (2015).

41 Fuller (1978) at 364 and 401.

42 A.M. Capron (1978) at 351.

43 As stressed by Lord Mance, "in order to account to the parties, and to enable them to assess whether to appeal where appropriate, our judgments must address the issues, they must explain to the parties why we have come to the conclusions we have on fact and law. They must cut to the chase, focusing on and analysing the points that matter, and not engaging in wide-ranging and unnecessary recitation or discourse, whether of fact or law" - J. M. Mance, 'The Role of Judges in a Representative Democracy', Lecture Given During the Judicial Committee of the Privy Council's Fourth Sitting in The Bahamas, 24 February 2017, paragraph 54.

44 Hodge (2021) at 147.

45 Eastman and Rix (2022); Kelly (2019).

46 A.M. Capron (2018) at S16.

concerning the issues examined. Judges, not elected through the democratic process, do not represent the lay public and are not accountable to the electorates for their decisions.[47] They are therefore not answerable to members of the public who are affected by their judgements.[48] Further, although judicial conduct is guided by the three basic principles of judicial independence, impartiality and integrity,[49] studies have shown that judges are not value free. Most judges come from an elite social background[50] and they may be influenced by their biases or belief-systems, and may also rely on intuition in their decision-making.[51] They are, in short, incapable of registering and reflecting the sentiments of the public which should arguably be the prime determinant of social policies embodied in laws.[52]

Reflecting upon the cases explored in the previous chapter, it can be observed that judges, through the judicial process, were only invited to adjudicate on a narrow set of circumstances. In the situations discussed, it was clear that the agenda also dictates how the decision was made. The question posed to the judges was whether a ventilated patient in ICU was dead and whether it would be lawful to withdraw their ventilation. Judges in turn perceived and framed their task as one to find out what are the criteria used by doctors to determine death, and whether these were satisfied in the circumstances. Thus rather than asking how should death be determined, or whether the definition and criteria used by the medical profession are sufficiently robust, their angle of inquiry saw to it that the diagnosis and criteria used by the Conference, and later the Academy, received legal endorsement. It also led to the exclusion of other alternative definitions and determinations of death. In this way, ventilators can be removed from patients who are brain stem dead even if they are considered still alive in other jurisdictions and from a religious perspective. Such an uncompromising stance is taken without being preceded or informed by its own independent research or of wider consultation or debate—as these are not, as mentioned above, within the scope of judicial decision-making.[53] Neither would the making of exceptions or reasonable accommodation be fitting, as they have a responsibility to ensure that the law is clear and consistent.[54]

Those cases were also deliberated upon on the basis of the facts immediately before the judges and they were meant to address only the concerns of the disputing parties. Yet as mentioned, their decisions can have wider implications. By recognising that brain stem dead patients are legally dead, the judiciary indirectly legitimised heart-beating organ donation since vital organs are retrieved from patients who are

[47] *R (on the Application of Nicklinson and Another) v. Ministry of Justice* [2014] UKSC 38, *per* Lord Neuberger at paragraph 104; Sumption (2011) at 303.

[48] Weiler (1970) at 6.

[49] Courts and Tribunal Judiciary (2020), pp. 6–8.

[50] Shetreet and Turenne (2013), p. 16; Grødeland and Miller (2015), pp. 275–276; Fouzder (2019).

[51] Donald et al. (2020–2021) at 76; Fouzder (2020); Rachlinski et al. (2008–2009) at 1197; Guthrie et al. (2007) at 3; Drobak and North (2008) at 138–140; Fleisher (2008) at 920.

[52] P. Weiler, op. cit. p. 6.

[53] A.M. Capron (1978), op. cit., 351.

[54] Engstad (2017), paragraph 6.

considered to have died. However, the rationale they gave for withdrawing ventilation from brain stem dead patients, namely to allow dignity in death, does not seem to sit comfortably with allowing the continuation of ventilation for purposes of heart-beating organ donation. This is especially so since the act of dissecting and removing multiple organs are even more intrusive than a mere continuation of ventilation, and these are performed for the benefit of other people.

A legitimacy forged through case law is therefore subject to the limitations of the judicial system. Yet judicial endorsement of DNC has far-reaching implications over matters that were not necessarily within the judges' contemplation when the cases were heard. In view of these shortcomings, attention is turned next to the comparative rigour and advantages of the legislative process.

4.4 Advantages of Parliamentary Law-Making

Parliamentary law-making, when contrasted to courtroom hearings, has the advantage of being more inclusive, capacitous and democratic. A law that is produced in Parliament can benefit from extensive and well-considered debates through the two houses of Parliament. Members of Parliament (MPs) in the House of Commons, unlike judges, represent the community at large, and thereby reflect the voice and opinion of the electorates.[55] The law can also benefit from the opinions and careful scrutiny of House of Lords' peers who bring a wide range of expertise and experience.[56] Unlike a courtroom, Parliament is less constrained by resources and time. During the Committee stage in both houses, detailed examination of a Bill can take place with evidence taken from a wide range of experts and stakeholders from outside Parliament.[57] This includes receiving written and oral evidence, as well as availing themselves of the works of academics and the wider research community.[58] This set up therefore allows for divergent viewpoints, and not just of those involved on either side of a court case, to be heard and considered.[59] It also has more capacity to contemplate on the wider implications of any decision being taken. All these make the Parliamentary process more apt than courtrooms to resolve controversial and complex issues triggered by moral and social dilemmas,[60] such as the present one.

---

[55] UK Parliament, 'House of Commons', available at https://www.parliament.uk/business/commons/.

[56] UK Parliament, 'Who's in the House of Lords', available at https://www.parliament.uk/business/lords/whos-in-the-house-of-lords/.

[57] UK Parliament, 'Committee Stage (Commons)', available at https://www.parliament.uk/about/how/laws/passage-bill/commons/coms-commons-comittee-stage/; UK Parliament, 'Committee Stage (Lords)', available at https://www.parliament.uk/about/how/laws/passage-bill/commons/coms-lords-committee-stage/.

[58] Rose et al. (2020) at 626–627.

[59] A.M. Capron (2018), op. cit., p. S16.

[60] *R (on the Application of Nicklinson and Another) v. Ministry of Justice* [2014] UKSC 38, per Lord Sumption at paragraph 232.

Indeed Lord Browne-Wilkinson suggested as much back in 1993 *in Airedale NHS Trust v. Bland*.[61] According to His Lordship, "[t]he ability to sustain life artificially is of relatively recent origin. Existing law may not provide an acceptable answer to the new legal questions which it raises. Should judges seek to develop new law to meet a wholly new situation? Or is this a matter which lies outside the area of legitimate development of the law by judges and requires society, through the democratic expression of its views in Parliament, to reach its decisions on the underlying moral and practical problems and then reflect those decisions in legislation? I have no doubt that it is for Parliament, not the courts, to decide the broader issues which [such] cases [raise]."[62]

It is important to emphasise that Parliamentary intervention at this stage is not to consider the acceptability of neurological death. The concept is now an entrenched part of the medico-legal discourse. Rather, it is an opportunity to debate and deliberate on at least the following issues: the robustness of the existing formulation and criteria of death; and the feasibility and significance of religious exemption in relation to the withdrawal of artificial ventilation.

As regards the robustness of the existing formulation and framework, one clear advantage of Parliamentary intervention is the ability to hear the testimony and evidence of various experts regarding DNC practices in different parts of the world. This could lead to informed and meaningful Parliamentary debates as to whether the definition, criteria and protocol currently adopted in the UK are sufficiently robust in comparison to those adopted elsewhere. Here, it is worth emphasising that the significance of the issue is not confined to ascertaining when mechanical ventilation can be withdrawn from brain stem dead patients, simply because this was the issue which came up in the courtroom. Having a robust DNC framework which benefits from democratic deliberation is also important because it would determine when vital organs can be removed from heart-beating donors.[63]

Connected to this, debates would need to consider the form that legislation should take: should Parliament set both the general legal standard and the medical criteria for determining neurological death; or only the former while leaving the latter to the medical profession?[64] How can it be ensured that the legal definition can continue to be responsive to advances in medical technology?[65] The legislative experience of other jurisdictions could be reflected on, including how they negotiate DNC's standing alongside the traditional cardio-respiratory standard for determining death.

The Parliamentary process could also give religious and other social groups an opportunity to voice their concerns.[66] Since the judiciary's one-size-fits-all approach which admits of no exception means that the UK's version of DNC is currently superimposed on those who do not subscribe to brain-based death on religious grounds,

---

[61] [1993] AC 789.

[62] At 878.

[63] Charters (2021).

[64] Skegg (1976) at 191; Omelianchuk et al. (2022); Pope (2018) at S47.

[65] Parent and Turi (2020) at E1055.

[66] Choong (2013) at 20.

the Parliamentary process can help ameliorate the adverse effect this continues to have on them. By listening to various stakeholders and by legislating on the matter, room can be created for an exemption when it comes to the withdrawal of ventilation and LST in ICUs and neurological centres. Parliament could safeguard their interests by reflecting on and adapting from the experiences of jurisdictions which currently make such provisions. This includes the legislative framework of New Jersey's Declaration of Death Act 1991 which had facilitated the continuation of LST for Jahi McMath when her family rejected her doctors' diagnosis of death and decision to terminate LST.[67] According to section 5 of the Act, "[t]he death of an individual shall not be declared upon the basis of neurological criteria when the licenced physician authorised to declare death, has reason to believe, on the basis of information in the individual's available medical records, or information provided by a member of the individual's family or any other person knowledgeable about the individual's personal religious beliefs that such a declaration would violate the personal religious beliefs of the individual. In these cases, death shall be declared, and the time of death fixed, solely upon the basis of cardio-respiratory criteria…". Following this provision, when a religious objection is made to the use of DNC, the patient is not considered legally dead unless and until there is an irreversible cessation of circulatory and respiratory functions.[68] It is necessary to highlight that the Act does not eliminate neurological death. It merely provides that this method for determining death be substituted with the long-established cardio-respiratory criteria—a method which is well-accepted by Abrahamic faith communities and is more sympathetic to their understanding of death. Further, section 7 of the Act prohibits any healthcare practitioner, provider, health service plan, insurer or governmental authority, from denying insurance and health benefits coverage for the continuation of life-support to those patients until their hearts stop beating. Thus the Act also safeguards funding when the provision of section 5 is invoked. Should a similar model be introduced in the UK, it could require the NHS to allow patients to remain ventilated until their hearts stop beating naturally in ICUs and neurological centres. As NHS care is publicly funded, part of the discussion that needs to take place during the legislative process is how these additional costs are shouldered.

Parliamentary debates could also extend to other closely connected issues. For instance, should exemptions only be recognised on religious grounds or should it be extended to moral, philosophical and other grounds? Should conscientious objection be recognised for healthcare practitioners who are unwilling to continue treating such patients after neurological death is confirmed? Should the exemption also apply for purposes of organ donation? Another significant matter is one which has surfaced in the *Battersbee* case where it was reported that his parents had at one point refused to allow his doctors to perform brain stem tests.[69] Hence if a religious exemption is recognised, should this extend to allowing family members to refuse such tests from being carried out? In fact, should such tests not be preceded by consent in

[67] Lewis et al. (2016) at 481.

[68] Johnson (2016) at 109.

[69] [2022] EWHC 1435 (Fam) at paragraph 16.

any event?[70] These are among the important issues that could be debated in the Parliamentary chambers, which courtrooms do not have the capacity for.

4.5 Conclusion

DNC gained legal recognition when the courts approved the definition of death and diagnostic criteria espoused by the Conference of the Medical Royal Colleges, and later the Codes of Practice issued by the Academy of Medical Royal Colleges and the Royal College of Paediatricians and Child Health. This has allowed doctors to legitimately withdraw artificial ventilation from brain stem dead patients treated in ICUs and neurological centres. This includes, without exception, patients who do not accept DNC as currently formulated by these professional bodies. This chapter has explored divergent views regarding the definition and diagnosis of death. This was looked at from a global perspective for the adopters of neurological death and from a religious perspective. As discussed, these issues were given insufficient legal consideration owing to the inherent limitations of the courtroom as a law-making forum.

Parliament, by contrast, has the capacity and resources to consider the 2 issues regarding diversity in the understanding and interpretation of death at length. It has the capacity to hear a wide range of viewpoints from medical experts to religious representatives and other stakeholders. This would allow a matter as important as when a human being in ICU dies, to be democratically decided rather than for it to be the preserve of the medical profession. Parliament also has the ability to recognise an exemption for those who do not agree that their deaths should be determined via DNC. This can be beneficial on several levels. It would allow religious communities to practise their faith in the final stage of their life in a matter as serious, private and personal as death.[71] This not only helps protect their religious concerns and welfare,[72] it could alleviate the tension and distrust often present in situations where doctors and family members hold discordant views.[73] After all, in publicly-funded NHS facilities, patients and their families do not have the luxury of selecting clinicians who share or understand their values.[74] An exemption could prevent additional anguish at a time when family members are wrestling with an impending loss and are at their most vulnerable.[75] It also obviates the need to go to court.[76] This is currently met by a

---

[70] T. Pope, op. cit., S47–S48; Johnson (2020) at 35.

[71] Delaney (2010) at 31.

[72] Choong and Rady (2018) at 86.

[73] Copnell (2014) at 261.

[74] Swanepoel (2022) at 3.

[75] Walker (2020).

[76] Choong (2022) at 112–113.

predictable outcome[77] and is also costly for the NHS, the family members and the taxpayers.[78] There are emotional costs too. Doctors involved in end-of-life cases, for instance, have found it difficult and stressful to be portrayed and experienced by family members as the enemy who need to be fought to save the life of their loved ones.[79] For family members, the pain and distress they already feel would no doubt be exacerbated when exposed to the further agony of hearing their loved ones being referred to repeatedly in court as already deceased, and perceived as a "loiterer" in the ICU.[80] Worse still, that their objection represents nothing other than an inability to let go or to confront reality.[81] A statutory recognition of a religious exemption could therefore protect and empower them in a meaningful way.[82]

References

Alexander, I. 2019. Humility Before New Scientific Evidence: We No Longer Have Moral Certainty That "Brain Death" is True Death. *The Linacre Quarterly* 86 (4): 314–326.
Alhawari, Y., et al. 2020. Religious Denomination Influencing Attitudes Towards Brain Death, Organ Transplantation and Autopsy—A Survey Among People of Different Religions. *International Journal of Legal Medicine* 134 (3): 1203–1212.
Ashkenazi, T., J. Lavee, and E. Mor. 2015. Organ Donation in Israel—Achievements and Challenges. *Transplantation* 99 (2): 265–266.
Bedir, A., and S. Aksoy. 2011. Brain Death Revisited: It Is Not 'Complete Death' According to Islamic Sources. *Journal of Medical Ethics* 37: 290–294.
Bible, Genesis 7:22.
Breshnahan, M.J., and K. Mahler. 2010. Ethical Debate Over Organ Donation in the Context of Brain Death'. *Bioethics* 24 (2): 54–60.
Cameron, E.J., et al. 2016. Confirmation of Brainstem Death. *Practical Neurology* 16, 129–135.
Canadian Catholic Bioethics Institute. Organ Donation: A Catholic Perspective.
Capron, A.M. 1978. Legal Definition of Death. *Annals of the New York Academy of Sciences* 315 (1): 349–362.
Capron, A.M. 2018. Beecher Dépassé: Fifty Years of Determining Death, Legally. *Hastings Center Report* 48 (6): S14–S18.
Charters, C. 2021. "Brain-Dead" Teenager, 18, Wakes Up. *The Times* 31 March.
Choong, K.A., and M.Y. Rady. 2018. Re A (A Child) and the United Kingdom Code of Practice for the Diagnosis and Confirmation of Death: Should a Secular Construct of Death Override Religious Values in a Pluralistic Society? *HEC Forum* 71–89.
Choong, K.A. 2013. Organ Procurement: A Case for Pluralism on the Definition of Death. *Journal of Medical Law and Ethics* 1 (1): 5–21.
Choong, K.A. 2020. Re M (Declaration of Death of Child) [2020]: "No Best Interests to Consider"? In *Culture and Law: Multidisciplinary Cross-Fertilization of Views on the End of Life*, ed. S. Rohlfing-Dijoux, and U. Hellmann, 105–114. Baden-Baden: Nomos. https://doi.org/10.5771/9783748921271-105.

[77] See discussion in Chap. 3.
[78] Son and Setta (2018).
[79] A. Swanepoel, op. cit., p. 3.
[80] Johnson (2014) at 35.
[81] See discussion in Chap. 3.
[82] Olick (1991) at 278.

Chua, H.C., et al. 2015. Brain Death: The Asian Perspective. *Journal of Medical Law and Ethics* 35 (2): 152–161.
Copnell, B. 2014. Brain Death: Lessons from the McMath Case. *American Journal of Critical Care* 23 (3): 259–262.
Courts and Tribunal Judiciary. 2020. Guide to Judicial Conduct (March).
Delaney, R. 2010. *Defining Death: Why All Fifty States Should Adopt the Uniform Definition of Death Act with a Religious Exception.* Marquette University Law School Legal Studies Research Paper Series, Research Paper No. 10-24.
Disney, L., and L. Poston. 2010. The Breath of Life: Christian Perspectives on Conception and Ensoulment. *Anglican Theological Review* 92 (2): 271–295.
Donald, B., J. Rachlinski, and A. Wistrich. 2020–2021 Getting Explicit About Implicit Bias *Judicature* 104 (3): 75–80.
Drobak, J.N., and D.C. North. 2008. Understanding Judicial Decision-Making: The Importance of Constraints on Non-rational Deliberations. *Journal of Law and Policy* 26: 131–152.
Eastman, N., and K. Rix. 2022. Bias in Expert Witness Practice: Sources, Routes to Expression and How to Minimise It. *BJ Psych Advances* 28 (1): 35–45.
Editorial. 2011. Religion, Organ Transplantation, and the Definition of Death. *The Lancet* 377: 271.
Engstad, N. 2017. Consistency of the Case Law as a Prerequisite to Legal Certainty: European and National Perspectives. In *Introduction at the High-Level Conference on the Harmonisation of Case Law and Judicial Practice*, Athens, 29 September 2017.
Fleisher, M. 2008. Judicial Decision Making Under the Microscope: Moving Beyond Politics Versus Precedent. *Rutgers University Law Review* 60 (4): 919–968.
Fouzder, M. 2019. Senior Judges "Most Socially Exclusive" of All. *The Law Society Gazette*, 25 June.
Fouzder, M. 2020. Judicial Induction Training to Tackle "Implicit Bias". *The Law Society Gazette*, 6 November.
Fuller, L. 1978. The Forms and Limits of Adjudication. *Harvard Law Review* 92: 353–409.
Gabbay, E., and J.J. Fins. 2019. Go in Peace: Brain Death, Reasonable Accommodation and Jewish Mourning Rituals. *Journal of Religion and Health* 58: 1672–1686.
Greer, D.M., et al. 2020. Determination of Brain Death/Death by Neurologic Criteria: The World Brain Death Project. *Journal of the American Medical Association* 324 (11): 1078–1097.
Grødeland, B., and W.L. Miller. 2015. *European Legal Cultures in Transition*. Cambridge: Cambridge University Press.
Guthrie, C., J.J. Rachlinski, and A.J., Wistrich. 2007. Blinking on the Bench: How Judges Decide Cases. *Cornell Law Review* 93 (1): 1–44.
Haas, J.M. 2011. Catholic Teaching Regarding the Legitimacy of Neurological Criteria for the Determination of Death. *The National Catholic Bioethics Quarterly* 279–299.
Herring, J. 2021. *Law Through the Life Course*. Bristol: Bristol University Press.
Hodge, P.S. 2021. The Scope of Judicial Law-Making in Constitutional and Public Law. *Judicial Review* 26 (2): 146–177.
Hussain, A. 2022. Is The "Concept" of Brain Death Compatible with "Reality" of "Religious Death". *Journal of the British Islamic Medical Association* 10 (4): 12–29.
Jacobovits, I.1980. Medicine and Judaism—An Overview. *Jewish Medical Ethics* 57–78.
Johnson, L.S.M. 2014. A Legal Fiction with Real Consequences. *American Journal of Bioethics* 14 (8): 34–36.
Johnson, L.S.M. 2016. The Case for Reasonable Accommodation of Conscientious Objections to Declarations of Brain Death. *Bioethical Inquiry* 13: 105–115.
Johnson, L.S.M. 2020. Restoring Trust and Requiring Consent in Death by Neurological Criteria. *American Journal of Bioethics* 20 (6): 33–35.
Jones, D.A. 2012. Loss of Faith in Brain Death: Catholic Controversy Over the Determination of Death by Neurological Criteria. *Clinical Ethics* 7 (3): 133–141.
Jütte, R. 2021. *The Jewish Body: A History*. Translated by E. Bredeck. Philadelphia: University of Pennsylvania Press.

Kelly, A. 2019. Medical Experts and Evaluations of the Standard of Care in Medical Litigation—Strengths, Weaknesses and Potential Improvement. *Journal of Law and Medicine* 27: 455–471.

Lewis, A., P. Varelas, and D. Greer. 2016. Prolonging Support After Brain Death: When Families Ask for More. *Neurocritical Care* 24, 481–487.

Lewis, A., et al. 2020. Determination of Death by Neurologic Criteria Around the World. *Neurology* 95: e299–e309.

Lock, M. 1996. Death in Technological Time: Locating the End of Meaningful Life. *Medical Anthropology Quarterly* 10 (4): 575–600.

Mance, J.M. 2017. The Role of Judges in a Representative Democracy. In Lecture Given During the Judicial Committee of the Privy Council's Fourth Sitting in The Bahamas, 24 February 2017, paragraph 54, available at https://www.supremecourt.uk/docs/speech-170224.pdf.

Miller, A.C. 2016. Opinions on the Legitimacy of Brain Death Among Sunni and Shi'a Scholars. *Journal of Religion and Health* 55: 394–402.

Moreland, J.P. *Restoring the Soul to Christianity*. Christian Research Institute, Statement DR502.

Napier, S. 2009. Brain Death A Morally Legitimate Criteria for Determining Death? *The Linacre Quarterly* 76 (1): 68–81.

Neudorf, L. 2015. Judicial Independence: The Judge as a Third Party to the Dispute. *Oxford University Comparative Law Forum* 2. Available at https://ouclf.law.ox.ac.uk/judicial-independence-the-judge-as-a-third-party-to-the-dispute/.

Nguyen, D. 2017. Pope John Paul II and the Neurological Standard for the Determination of Death: A Critical Analysis of His Address to the Transplantation Society. *The Linacre Quarterly* 84 (2): 155–186.

O'Rourke, K.D., and P.J. Boyle. 2011. *Medical Ethics: Sources of Catholic Teachings*. Washington: Georgetown University Press.

Olick, R.S. 1991. Brain Death, Religious Freedom, and Public Policy: New Jersey's Landmark Legislative Initiative. *Kennedy Institute of Ethics Journal* 1 (4): 275–288.

Omelianchuk, A., et al. 2022. Revise the Uniform Determination of Death Act to Align the Law with Practice Through Neurorespiratory Criteria. *Neurology* 98, 532–536.

Padela, A.I., A. Arozullah, and E. Moosa. 2013. Brain Death in Islamic Ethico-Legal Deliberation: Challenges for Applied Islamic Bioethics. *Bioethics* 27 (3): 132–139.

Parent, B., and A. Turi. 2020. Death's Troubled Relationship with the Law. *AMA Journal of Ethics* 22 (12): E1055–E1061.

Pope, T. 2018. Brain Death and the Law: Hard Cases and Legal Challenges. *Hastings Center Report* 48 (6): S46–S48.

Quran, Surah Al-Maidah: verse 32.

Quran, Surah As-Sajdah: verse 9.

Rachlinski, J.J., et al. 2008–2009. Does Unconscious Racial Bias Affect Trial Judges? *Notre Dame Law Review* 84, 1195–1246.

Rady, M.Y., and J.L. Verheijde. 2013. Brain-Dead Patients Are Not Cadavers: The Need to Revise the Definition of Death in Muslim Communities. *HEC Forum* 25: 25–45.

Robbins, N.M. and J.L. Bernat. 2018. When Do You Order Ancillary Tests to Determine Brain Death? *Neurology Clinical Practice* 8 (3): 266–274.

Rose, D.C., et al. 2020. Improving the Use of Evidence in Legislatures: The Case of the UK Parliament. *Evidence and Policy* 16 (4): 619–638.

Setta, S.M., and S.D. Shemie. 2015. An Explanation and Analysis of How World Religions Formulate Their Ethical Decisions on Withdrawing Treatment and Determining Death. *Philosophy, Ethics, and Humanities in Medicine* 10 (6). https://doi.org/10.1186/s13010-015-0025-x.

Shemie, S.D., et al. 2014. International Guideline Development for the Determination of Death. *Intensive Care Medicine* 40: 788–797.

Shetreet, S., and S. Turenne. 2013. *Judges on Trial: The Independence and Accountability of the English Judiciary*. Cambridge: Cambridge University Press.

Shewmon, D.A. 1998. "Brainstem Death," "Brain Death" and Death: A Critical Re-evaluation of the Purported Equivalence. *Issues in Law and Medicine* 14 (2): 125–145.

Shomali, M.A. 2008. Islamic Bioethics: A General Scheme. *Journal of Medical Ethics and History of Medicine* 1.

Skegg, P.D.G. 1976. The Case for a Statutory Definition of Death. *Journal of Medical Ethics* 190–192.

Smith, M. 2012. Brain Death: Time for an International Consensus. *British Journal of Anaesthesia* 108 (S1): i6–i9.

Son, R.G., and S.M. Setta. 2018. Frequency of Use of the Religious Exemption in New Jersey Cases of Determination of Brain Death. *19 BMC Medical Ethics*. https://doi.org/10.1186/s12910-018-0315-0.

Spears, W., A. Mian, and D.M. Greer. 2022. Brain Death: A Clinical Overview. *Journal of Intensive Care* 10. https://doi.org/10.1186/s40560-022-00609-4.

Sprung, C.L., et al. 2014. Seeking Worldwide Professional Consensus on the Principles of End-of-Life Care for the Critically Ill: The Consensus for Worldwide End-of Life Practice for Patients in Intensive Care Units (WELPICUS) Study. *American Journal of Respiratory and Critical Care Medicine* 190 (8): 855–866.

Sumption, J. 2011. Judicial and Political Decision-Making: The Uncertain Boundary. *Judicial Review* 16 (4): 301–315.

Swanepoel, A. 2022. Fifteen-Minute Consultation: How to Communicate with Parents Who Have a Child on Life Support With No Hope of Recovery. *Archives of Disease in Childhood: Education and Practice Edition* 1–6.

Talmud, Yoma: 85a.

Tendler, M.D. 1996. *Responsa of Rav Moshe Feinstein: Translation and Commentary (Volume 1: Care of the Critically Ill)*. New Jersey: KTAV Publishing House Inc.

UK Parliament. House of Commons. Available at https://www.parliament.uk/business/commons/.

UK Parliament. Who's in the House of Lords. Available at https://www.parliament.uk/business/lords/whos-in-the-house-of-lords/.

UK Parliament. Committee Stage (Commons). Available at https://www.parliament.uk/about/how/laws/passage-bill/commons/coms-commons-committee-stage/.

UK Parliament. Committee Stage (Lords). Available at https://www.parliament.uk/about/how/laws/passage-bill/commons/coms-lords-committee-stage/.

Verheijde, J.L., and M. Potts. 2010. Commentary on the Concept of Brain Death Within the Catholic Bioethical Framework. *Christian Bioethics* 16 (3): 246–256.

Verheijde, J.L., M.Y. Rady, and M. Potts. 2018. Neuroscience and Brain Death Controversies: The Elephant in the Room. *Journal of Religion and Health* 57, 1745–1763.

Walker, A. 2020. Parents of Brain-Damaged Baby Lose Life Support Legal Battle. *The Guardian*, 14 February.

Weiler, P. 1970. Legal Values and Judicial Decision-Making. *The Canadian Bar Review* XLVIII, 1–46.

Chapter 5
General Conclusion

Abstract Diagnosis of death using neurological criteria is a construct which has been part of the clinical practice in the UK for nearly half a century. It has also been continuously endorsed by the judiciary during that period. This chapter looks back at its medico-legal journey to date, before looking ahead to the future.

Keywords Academy of Medical Royal Colleges · Brain stem death · Judges · Case law · Statutory definition of death · Parliament

5.1 Introduction

Ushered in enthusiastically by the medical profession and accepted approvingly by the judiciary, diagnosis of death by neurological criteria has been part of the British medico-legal landscape for nearly half a century. This chapter looks back at its emergence and ascendancy, before looking ahead to the future.

5.2 Past to Present: A Summary

5.2.1 The Medical Context

DNC is a construct which owes its origin to the rising use of mechanical ventilation within modern ICUs. As discussed in Chap. 1, it began as a quest for diagnostic criteria, the satisfaction of which had been used by two French neurophysiologists to justify the discontinuation of what could otherwise be an indeterminate prolongation of life for patients who were in a state they called *coma dépassé*. Since it was believed that such patients would never regain consciousness, the futility of the endeavour was therefore tendered as the rationale for the withdrawal of ventilation and all other LSTs. Before long, this state was re-described as brain death in the USA and it metamorphosised into a new definition of death. The criteria for its diagnosis and confirmation were outlined in 1968 in the *Report of the Ad Hoc Committee of the Harvard Medical School to Examine the Definition of Brain Death*. When these were

K. A. Choong, *The Medico-Legal Development of Neurological Death in the UK*,
https://doi.org/10.1007/978-981-19-6763-4_5

met, artificial ventilation could be removed on the basis that the person was already dead. There is therefore a paradigm shift involved. When justifying the removal of ventilation on the grounds of futility, this was from patients who were deemed as still being alive. Whereas in the latter, brain death represents or is tantamount to, death. Once this diagnosis was made, the body of the ventilated patient is perceived as a cadaver and a corpse. This brings to an end any existing duty to provide medical treatment to the patient, and ventilation could be withdrawn. Vital organs could also be removed while ventilation was ongoing without contravening the dead donor rule.

Diagnosis of death using brain-based criteria has since gained acceptance in many countries around the world. In the UK, efforts in this direction were, as highlighted in Chap. 2, spearheaded by the Conference of Medical Royal Colleges and Their Faculties. Known as the Academy of Medical Royal Colleges since 1996, this is the membership body for the UK and Ireland's 24 medical royal colleges and faculties.[1] In 1976, the Conference declared that permanent functional death of the brain stem represented brain death. When the conditions and criteria it outlined for the diagnosis and confirmation of brain death were met, ventilatory support should be removed as this was no longer benefitting the patient. Brain death was therefore viewed as a condition indicative of futility or a very poor clinical prognosis. A patient with this diagnosis was accordingly deemed dying, hence alive, rather than dead.

However, the Conference revised its position just 3 years later. In 1979, it was announced that brain death represented the stage at which the patient becomes truly dead. This was on the grounds that all functions of the brain have by then permanently and irreversibly ceased. Since this proclamation was not accompanied by any changes in the criteria introduced in 1976 to diagnose brain death, the criteria previously used for prognostic purposes were now used for diagnosing death in adult ICUs and neurological centres. This was not only for the purposes of withdrawing ventilation and all LST in order to allow the body to be handed back to the family. This was also, as made clear by the *Code of Practice for the Removal of Cadaveric Organs for Transplantation* issued by the Health Departments of Great Britain and Northern Ireland in that same year, the case for the removal of cadaveric organs for transplantation. This document, which was later updated in 1983, specified that death for purposes of organ donation could also now (in addition to the traditional cardiac-based criteria) be diagnosed by reference to the irreversible cessation of brain stem function ('brain death'). This state is to be determined through application of the criteria outlined by the Conference. Once these are met, it was said that it is ethical to maintain ventilation for eligible donors until organ removal is complete. Then in 1991, the British Paediatric Association recommended that those criteria now used to determine death for adults in ICUs and neurological centres also apply to children over 2 months old who are comatose, totally apnoeic and being ventilated.

In 1995, the Conference endorsed a Review by a Working Group convened by the RCP. The Working Group provided a definition of death, which is the irreversible loss of the capacity for consciousness, combined with irreversible loss of the capacity to breathe. Given that the irreversible cessation of brain stem function will produce this

[1] Academy of Medical Royal Colleges, 'About us', https://www.aomrc.org.uk/about-us/.

clinical state, it was emphasised that brain stem death is equivalent to the death of the individual. In line with this, the Review suggested that the term "brain death" should be replaced by "brain stem death", while no change was recommended to the clinical criteria for diagnosing brain stem death. In 1998, the recommendations of the 1995 Review were incorporated into a new code of practice. Issued by the Academy of Medical Royal Colleges, the *Code of Practice for the Diagnosis of Brain Stem Death: Including Guidelines for the Identification and Management of Potential Organ and Tissue Donors* updated the Conference's 1976 and 1979 documents, and the Health Departments' 1983 Code of Practice. According to the Code, when the brain stem of a coma patient has been damaged in such a way and to such an extent that its functions are irreversibly destroyed, this condition is described as brain stem death. The criteria for establishing this are as per those originally set out in the Conference's 1976 document. Once these criteria are met, the patient is dead and this brings to an end any duty of care on the part of his/her doctors to provide further medical treatment. Artificial ventilation can be withdrawn. At that point, it is also apparently proper to consider whether any of the now deceased person's organs can be made available for transplantation. If so, the deceased's body can continue to be ventilated so as to enable and facilitate heart-beating organ donation. By bringing into one document the issue of how brain stem death should be diagnosed, with guidelines for the management of potential organ and tissue donors, the Code continued the pattern set by the 1979 and 1983 Codes of Practice. Together, they reveal and illustrate the presence of a unique relationship between the new definition of death and the field of organ transplantation.

The Academy has since issued *The Code of Practice for the Diagnosis and Confirmation of Death* in 2008. This represents the Academy's latest and thereby current guidelines. It is applicable to adults and children over 2 months old. The Academy affirmed the definition of death as the irreversible loss of the capacity for consciousness, combined with irreversible loss of the capacity to breathe. They likewise affirmed that the irreversible cessation of brain stem function will produce this clinical state. Patients with this condition are no longer able to breathe unaided without ventilatory support, and this loss of function is irreversible and permanent. A brain stem dead patient is therefore clinically dead. While the Academy admits that this state does not entail the cessation of all neurological activity in the brain, it highlighted that any potential activities are not indicative of any form of consciousness linked with human life. Similarly, while some residual reflex movement of the limbs may be present, this is controlled through the spinal cord rather than the brain.

According to the Code of Practice, the following 3 conditions must be satisfied before a diagnosis of death using neurological criteria can be undertaken: the patient's condition is undoubtedly due to irreversible brain damage of known aetiology; the patient is deeply comatose, unresponsive and apnoeic, with his/her lungs being artificially ventilated; and the patient is maintained on ventilatory support because spontaneous respiration has ceased. The Code also endorsed and reconfirmed the criteria previously outlined by the Conference relating to the diagnosis of death following irreversible cessation of brain stem function. To ensure that brain stem reflexes are absent: the pupils are fixed in diameter and do not respond to sharp changes in the intensity of incident light; there is no corneal reflex; the ocular-vestibular reflexes are absent; no motor responses within the cranial nerve distribution can be elicited by adequate stimulation of any somatic area; there is no cough reflex response to bronchial stimulation by a suction catheter placed down the trachea to the carina, or gag response to stimulation of the posterior pharynx with a spatula; and the process for testing the respiratory response to hypercarbia (apnoea test) should be the last brain stem reflex to be tested and should not be performed if any of the preceding tests confirm the presence of brain stem reflexes. The Code further stated that brain stem testing to diagnose death should be conducted by at least 2 medical practitioners who have been registered for more than 5 years. One of whom must be a Consultant. While they must be competent in the conduct and interpretation of brain stem testing, none of them should be a member of the transplant team. A complete set of tests should be carried out on 2 occasions by the 2 doctors acting together. Death is confirmed upon the conclusion of the second test.

The concept of brain stem death is considered inappropriate for those below 37 weeks of gestation. As regards those between 37 weeks of corrected gestation (post menstrual) to 2 months old, the Royal College of Paediatrics and Child Health (RCPCH) published *The Diagnosis of Death by Neurological Criteria in Infants Less Than Two Months Old: Updated Recommendations* in 2015. This replaced its Working Party Report of 1991. According to the RCPCH, the preconditions outlined in the Academy's 2008 Code of Practice should be satisfied before diagnosing brain stem death. Hence the patient must be comatose and was artificially ventilated for apnoea; and the diagnosis of structural brain damage has been made or the immediate cause of coma is known. The following preconditions were added: that in post-asphyxiated infants or those who received intensive care after resuscitation, there should at least be 24 h of observation during which the preconditions crucial for assessment of DNC should be present before clinical testing is conducted for DNC. The period of observation may be extended in situations where there are concerns relating to residual drug-induced sedation. The RCPCH confirmed that the criteria for diagnosing brain stem death outlined in the Academy's 2008 Code of Practice can be used for infants in this age group absent brain stem reflexes; absent motor responses and where there is no respiratory response to hypercarbia. However, the following precautionary measures should be considered for the apnoea test: the use of a stronger hypercarbic stimulus in order to establish respiratory unresponsiveness. As in the case of those aged 2 months and above, 2 tests must be conducted in total. These are to be undertaken by 2 paediatricians who have been registered for more than 5 years and are competent in the procedure. One of whom should be a Consultant and they should undertake the testings together.

As seen, the 2008 Code of Practice represented the culmination of a still ongoing journey which began over 4 decades ago. Unlike the 1998 Code of Practice which preceded it, it does not deal directly with transplantation. The Academy emphasised that there is no logical relationship between DNC and organ donation. By making the assertion at this stage of DNC's developmental journey, when its association with organ transplantation was discernible in earlier documents, a conscious effort seemed to have been made to downplay or deny the link. This is presumably to stifle criticism and dampen fear that DNC may have been adopted for the purpose of increasing the availability of vital organs for transplantation.

5.2.2 The Legal Context

If organ transplantation may have played a part in DNC's development in the medical context, this does not seem to be the case for its legal journey. As discussed in Chap. 3, the jointly heard cases of *R v. Malcherek, R v. Steel*[2] gained DNC its legal recognition. Decided just 2 years after the Conference's 1979 Addendum was published, the court showed no hesitation in accepting that brain death, the term used then, equated the death of the person. Hence when doctors removed ventilators from patients diagnosed with this condition, it was held that this did not break the chain of causation from the initial attack which led to their being hospitalised and ventilated in the first place, with their death. In other words, it was accepted that the patients were already dead when the ventilators were removed. Or, to put it another way, it was not the termination of the ventilator which caused those patients' death, as they were already deemed dead when this happened. Through this, the court endorsed the Conference's stance on brain death and the criteria used for diagnosing the condition.

In 1993, when the House of Lords made references in *Airedale NHS Trust v. Bland*[3] that the medical profession has now accepted that death can be determined using brain-based criteria, these have been treated by lower courts as legal endorsement at the highest level. This elevated what were originally *obiter dicta*, given that Anthony Bland's brain stem was still alive, to a binding precedent. Thus in the years that follow, it is hardly surprising that the legal status of DNC is deemed settled. Subsequent cases seemed to accept neurological death without question. Brain stem death, the term now used in line with the recommendations of the medical profession, was considered applicable when determining death in both civil law and criminal law contexts.

When cases now come before the courts for a declaration as to whether a patient treated in an ICU has died and whether ventilation can thereby be removed, the judiciary frame their task as one to determine if the patient has died according to the definition and criteria set out by the medical profession. These are, today, those outlined in the Academy's 2008 Code of Practice and where relevant, the RCPCH's 2015 Guidance. Provided a diagnosis of death was made by reference to these documents, the courts are satisfied that death has occurred. With this, it is clear that the judiciary are content to leave the matter of how death is defined and determined to the medical profession. The only point on which they part company is in relation to the time of death. As for the 2 tests which the professional bodies have specified for diagnosing brain stem death, courts have proclaimed the conclusion of the first test as the legal time of death. Upon its confirmation, the ventilated patient is said to

---

[2] (1981) 73 Cr. App. R. 173.

[3] [1993] AC 789.

no longer have any best interests that need to be protected. They nevertheless have an interest in not having their bodies subjected to indignity. One source of indignity is the continuation of artificial ventilation of what the courts have, by that stage, considered as a dead body or a corpse. When a declaration is made, the following structure and forms of words are prescribed: expressly declare that the patient has died at a particular time and date; then give permission and declare that it is lawful for mechanical ventilation and other clinical interventions to be withdrawn; and identify that the purpose of the declaration was to allow the patient who had died "dignity in death".

By recognising that a brain stem dead patient is legally dead, this not only legalises the withdrawal of ventilation from such patients. It also enables the removal of vital organs from their ventilated bodies since heart-beating organ donation would not contravene the dead donor rule. That this is the case is an extension, albeit unplanned, of the courts' rulings. On the one hand, this indicates that unlike the emergence of the medical definition of death, the legal endorsement of DNC does not seem entangled with nor influenced by a desire to advance organ transplantation. However, if the courts held that there is dignity in death, and continuation of ventilation on a deceased person is an undignified imposition, the preservation of heartbeat and circulation via ventilation until organs are harvested would need to be justified.[4] Since none of the cases considered thus far were factually and directly concerned with organ donation, the justification has never had to be contemplated before. That, incidentally, was not the only issue which has not been, or could not be, properly considered by judges in their deliberations. Of greater significance is the fact that by viewing their task as one to ascertain whether the patient has died in accordance with the criteria accepted by doctors, this angle of inquiry led not only to the rubber-stamping of the clinical definition of death. It also prevents consideration of alternative and competing definitions of death. These shortcomings, as suggested in Chap. 4, could be alleviated through legislative intervention.

5.3 The Future of Death

It is interesting to note that regulation was regarded, in the early days of DNC, as "unnecessary and potentially counterproductive".[5] Rather, a "more flexible code of practice which responds to medical opinion and which would be interpreted in good faith"[6] was considered to be preferable. However, changes that have since taken place may make it necessary to revisit this viewpoint.

---

[4] Although the Health Departments' 1979 and 1983 Codes of Practice (at paragraphs 33 and 34 respectively) stated that it is ethical to maintain artificial ventilation and heartbeat until organ removal has been completed, no explanation was provided as to why this is the case.

[5] Kennedy (1977) at 5.

[6] Ibid., p. 6.

As highlighted in Chap. 2, codes of practice which have been issued in the last 4 decades have not always been consistent in their association with or dissociation from organ procurement. While a strong connection between organ transplant and DNC has been alluded to at the outset, this has subsequently been downplayed and eventually even denied. This lack of consistency can continue to cast doubt over whether the profession is always acting in good faith in relation, particularly, to the issue of whether neurological death was developed to advance organ transplantation or that the benefit which the transplantation field derives is purely coincidental and a by-product of the new definition of death.

In addition, almost half a century have elapsed since the 1979 Addendum. The NHS is now is serving a more heterogenous population.[7] Some from the Abrahamic faith traditions and other religious beliefs do not agree with neurological death nor heart-beating organ donation, notwithstanding the fact that many of their co-religionists may accept these. For them, a brain stem dead person on ventilatory support may still be considered alive as their breath is still maintained. This has led to a number of objections being contested in the courtroom. However, exactly how many similar cases there are that have not been brought to court remains unknown. As for those fought in court, they have all thus far been unsuccessful despite the potential merits of their claims.

Further, the law and policy on organ donation have moved to an opt out framework in the last decade—from the Human Transplantation (Wales) Act 2013 to the Organ Donation (Deemed Consent) Act 2019 in England and the Human Tissue (Authorisation) (Scotland) Act 2019, and now the Organ and Tissue Donation (Deemed Consent) Act (Northern Ireland) 2022.[8] This framework operates on the basis that anyone deemed suitable to be a cadaveric organ donor is presumed to have consented to a postmortem removal of their organs for transplantation, unless they took active measures to register their dissent whilst alive[9] or they are within one of the excluded groups recognised by law. This means that organ donation bears strong and direct implications for everyone. They would either have to actively make known their objection to being a donor, or be deemed to have consented to be one. For those who dies as a result of brain injury and who are on ventilators, this opens up the possibility of heart-beating organ donation if they have not opted out or are not in a legally excluded group. Members of faith communities who do not accept brain stem death certainly have a choice to opt out. However, this is only a meaningful choice if they are aware of how their death would be determined should they die while needing ventilatory support. For this, they need to be informed that organ procurement from such patients do not proceed on the basis that their heartbeat and breathing have ceased, but that their brain stem have died.[10] Public education and transparency are

---

[7] Choudry et al. (2018) at 23; Randhawa and Gardiner (2022) at 12.

[8] This will come into force in Spring 2023. See NHS Blood and Transplant, 'Organ Donation Law in Northern Ireland', available at https://www.organdonation.nhs.uk/uk-laws/organ-donation-law-in-northern-ireland/.

[9] Tennankore et al. (2021); Pieri and Metcalfe (2020) at 242; Albertsen (2018).

[10] Potts and Evans (2005) at 408.

very important[11] so that action or inaction as regards the new presumed consent policy is made on an informed basis. It is encouraging that the NHS has pledged to be faith-sensitive on the matter of organ donation not least by allowing people to specify that they would like the NHS to speak to their family or anyone else appropriate about how organ donation can go ahead in line with their faith or religious belief.[12] However, how far this involves a discussion about how death is defined remains unclear.

Furthermore, there are now more countries that have adopted neurological death compared to the 1970s. The fact that they do not all use the same criteria raise important questions. Are the formulation, criteria and protocol for diagnosing death in the UK sufficiently robust? Is there not a need for these to be subjected to critical scrutiny and democratic deliberation, rather than viewing the matter as the exclusive preserve of the medical profession? This is especially so since, as mentioned earlier, there seems to be an association between the new definition of death with organ transplantation. Finding a version of DNC which is democratically agreed is arguably just as important, if not more so, for the purposes of organ donation, than for the purposes of withdrawal of ventilation in ICUs. After all, ventilation and LST can already be lawfully withdrawn from living patients if their continuation is assessed as futile[13]—hence not just when, or until, patients are diagnosed as dead. Indeed, the *Battersbee* case is the most recent reminder of this.[14] Whereas for organ donation, heart-beating organ donation can only proceed after the patient is diagnosed dead. If the formulation and criteria used are not sufficiently robust, vital organs may be removed prematurely without public discussion and consensus.

The discussion in Chap. 4 has highlighted the comparative advantages and benefits of engaging the Parliamentary process, over judicial ruling, for the definition of death. It has the ability, among others, to listen to various experts including those from other jurisdictions. It also allows various stakeholders to be involved in the matter. The aim is to arrive democratically at a DNC formulation that is robust. An Act of Parliament is also able to provide an exemption to those who object to DNC, not just for the purposes of withdrawal of ventilation, but perhaps also for purposes of organ donation.

Ultimately, for DNC to gain more public confidence, there should ideally be a global consensus regarding how brain-based death is determined.[15] As highlighted in the previous chapter, there are variability and inconsistency in concepts, criteria and

---

[11] J.M. Pieri and N.H. Metcalfe, op. cit. pp. 246–247; Choong (2014) at 33.

[12] NHS Blood and Transplant, 'Get the Facts About Organ Donation', available at https://www.organdonation.nhs.uk/helping-you-to-decide/about-organ-donation/get-the-facts/.

[13] See e.g. *An NHS Trust and Others v. Y and Another* [2018] UKSC 46; *Aintree v. University Hospitals NHS Foundation Trust v. James* [2013] UKSC 67; *Great Ormond Street Hospital v. Yates, Gard and Gard* [2017] EWHC 1909 (Fam); *Alder Hey Children's NHS Foundation Trust v. Evans, James and Evans* [2018] EWHC 953 (Fam).

[14] *Dance and Battersbee v. Barts Health NHS Trust and Battersbee* [2022] EWCA Civ 1055; Supreme Court (2022).

[15] Al-Bar and Chamsi-Palla (2015), p. 239; Sprung et al. (2014) at 863.

protocols across the world. The lack of uniformity means that the same physiological condition may give rise to separate diagnoses and outcomes. To put it crudely, a patient who would be declared dead in one jurisdiction could still be alive in another.[16] To be simultaneously dead and alive[17] is obviously a highly awkward and undesirable situation. Whether someone is dead should not be dependent on the jurisdiction in which they reside or to which they have travelled.[18] Even when international consensus is achieved, it needs to be remembered that while DNC is widely accepted, it has never been universally supported.[19] For that reason, exemptions should still be recognised in domestic legislation for those who object to DNC on religious and other recognised grounds. They should instead be allowed to be declared dead by the more universally accepted circulatory-respiratory criteria.[20]

References

Academy of Medical Royal Colleges. About us. https://www.aomrc.org.uk/about-us/.

Al-Bar, M.A., and H. Chamsi-Palla. 2015. *Contemporary Bioethics: Islamic Perspective*. London: Springer Open.

Albertsen, A. 2018. Deemed Consent: Assessing the New Opt-Out Approach to Organ Procurement in Wales. *Journal of Medical Ethics*. https://doi.org/10.1136/medethics-2017-104475.

Choong, K.A. 2014. Losing Faith in the Dead Donor Rule. *Journal of Medical Law and Ethics* 2 (2–3): 23–35.

Choudry, M., A. Latif, and K.G. Warburton. 2018. An Overview of the Spiritual Importance of End-of-Life Care Among the Five Major Faiths in the United Kingdom. *Clinical Medicine* 18 (1): 23–31.

Goldsmith, J.L. 2007. Wanted! Dead and/or Alive: Choosing Among the Not-So-Uniform Statutory Definitions of Death. *University of Miami Law Review* 871–930.

Johnson, L.S.M. 2017. Death by Neurological Criteria: Expert Definitions and Lay Misgivings. *QJM: An International Journal of Medicine* 110 (5): 267–270.

Kennedy, I. 1977. The Definition of Death. *Journal of Medical Ethics* 3 (1): 5–6.

Lewis, A., et al. 2020. Determination of Death by Neurologic Criteria Around the World. *Neurology* 95: e299–e309.

NHS Blood and Transplant. *Get the Facts About Organ Donation*. Available at https://www.organdonation.nhs.uk/helping-you-to-decide/about-organ-donation/get-the-facts/.

NHS Blood and Transplant. *Organ Donation Law in Northern Ireland*. Available at https://www.organdonation.nhs.uk/uk-laws/organ-donation-law-in-northern-ireland/.

Pieri, J.M., and N.H. Metcalfe. 2020. The Organ Donation (Deemed Consent) Act 2019. *InnovAit* 13 (4): 242–248.

Pope, T.M. 2014. Legal Briefing: Brain Death and Total Brain Failure. *Journal of Clinical Ethics* 25 (3): 245–257.

Potts, M., and D.W. Evans. 2005. Does it Matter that Organ Donors are Not Dead? Ethical and Policy Implications. *Journal of Medical Ethics* 31: 406–409.

---

[16] Lewis et al. (2020) at e307.

[17] Goldsmith (2007) at 876.

[18] Ross (2018) at S53.

[19] Pope (2014) at 253.

[20] Shewmon (2021), p. 21; Johnson (2017) at 269.

Randhawa, G., and D. Gardiner. 2022. Tackling Organ Donation Among Minority Ethnic Communities in the UK—A Whole Systems Approach. *British Medical Bulletin* 142: 4–14.
Ross, L.F. 2018. Respecting Choice in Definitions of Death. *Hastings Center Report* 48 (6): S53–S55.
Shewmon, D.A. 2021. Statement in Support of Revising the Uniform Determination of Death Act and in Opposition to a Proposed Revision. *Journal of Medicine and Philosophy*. https://doi.org/10.1093/jmp/jhab014.
Sprung, C.L., et al. 2014. Seeking Worldwide Professional Consensus on the Principles of End-of-Life Care for the Critically Ill. *American Journal of Respiratory and Critical Care Medicine* 190 (8): 855–866.
Supreme Court. 2022. Permission to Appeal Decision in the Matter of Archie Battersbee, July 28. Available at https://www.supremecourt.uk/news/permission-to-appeal-decision-in-the-matter-of-archie-battersbee.html.
Tennankore, K.K., S. Klarenbach, and A. Goldberg. 2021. Perspectives on Opt-Out Versus Opt-In Legislation for Deceased Organ Donation: An Opinion Piece. *Canadian Journal of Kidney Health and Disease* 8: 1–6.

Correction to: The Medico-Legal Development of Neurological Death in the UK

Correction to:
K. A. Choong, *The Medico-Legal Development of Neurological Death in the UK*,
https://doi.org/10.1007/978-981-19-6763-4

In the original version of the book, the corrections received during the proof stage have been incorporated in the XML to view on the Springer Link. The correction chapters have been updated with the changes.

The updated original version of the book can be found at
https://doi.org/10.1007/978-981-19-6763-4

K. A. Choong, *The Medico-Legal Development of Neurological Death in the UK*,
https://doi.org/10.1007/978-981-19-6763-4_6

Index

K. A. Choong, *The Medico-Legal Development of Neurological Death in the UK*,
https://doi.org/10.1007/978-981-19-6763-4